THE LIFE OF
Beethoven

Hamlyn
London · New York · Sydney · Toronto

THE LIFE OF
Beethoven

Alan Kendall

To John Lavender

Published 1978 by
The Hamlyn Publishing Group Limited
London   New York   Sydney   Toronto
Astronaut House, Hounslow Road
Feltham, Middlesex

ISBN 0 600 31431 6

Printed in Spain
By Mateu Cromo Artes Gráficas S.A., Madrid

Phototypeset by Tradespools Ltd, Frome, Somerset

Contents

Bonn 1770

LUDWIG VAN BEETHOVEN was born in Bonn, on 15 or 16 December 1770. He was the son of Johann van Beethoven, a musician in the service of the Elector of Cologne, and the grandson of Ludwig van Beethoven, a musician at the same court, who had gone to Bonn from Malines as a young man.

The Electors of Cologne were also the archbishops, but since the mid-thirteenth century they had resided in Bonn, an attractive little city up river on the Rhine. In fact they had virtually no power in Cologne itself, which was a free city of the empire of which they were electors. The capital of that empire, Vienna, was the scene of Beethoven's professional career, but how much Bonn meant to him is made clear from a letter to his friend Franz Gerhard Wegeler, written when he was thirty-one, which makes him sound like an exile on an alien shore. It adds to our impression of Vienna as the background – whether native or adopted – of such famous men as Gluck, Mozart, Haydn, Beethoven, Schubert, and many others.

> My fatherland, the beautiful country in which
> I first saw the light of day, appears before me
> as vividly and as lovely as when I left you. The
> day that I am able to see you again and greet
> our Father Rhine I shall look upon as one of
> the happiest in my life. As to when that will be
> I cannot yet tell you.
>
> *Ludwig van Beethoven writing from Vienna to*
> *Franz Gerhard Wegeler in Bonn, 29 June 1801*

Some eight or nine years before he wrote this letter, Beethoven had left his native city of Bonn, for the second time, to study in Vienna. Though he could not have known it at the time, or even when he came to write the letter, he would never return to Bonn, and when he left it in 1792 the Elector of Cologne–whose subject the composer was–had less than two years in which to continue as ruler of his territory. And yet here was Beet-

Bonn Cathedral, whose school the young Ludwig van Beethoven attended, according to the Fischer manuscript. It is also possible that Zenser, the cathedral organist, gave him lessons; far more important as a teacher was the court organist, C. G. Neefe.

hoven writing from Vienna, the capital of the Holy Roman Empire as ruled over by the Hapsburg emperors, and Bonn was the administrative capital and seat of the ruler of a part of that empire. How, then, did Beethoven come to think of Bonn as being so very different from, and preferable to, Vienna where, at the time of writing, he had lived for over eight years, and where he was to be based for the rest of his life?

Basically the Holy Roman Empire, created when Charlemagne was crowned emperor on Christmas Day 800, was the successor in the West to the ancient Roman Empire. After many vicissitudes the territory that constituted the Holy Roman Empire became a federation of literally hundreds of independent sovereign states owing various degrees of allegiance to the elected emperors who, in the last phase of the empire's existence, were of the Hapsburg family centred on Vienna.

Those who elected the emperors were the archbishops of Trier, Mainz and Cologne, and the electors of Bohemia, the Palatinate of the Rhine, Saxony and Brandenburg in the first instance, with the later addition of Bavaria and Hanover. This curious mixture of the sacred and the secular by no means seemed strange to either governors or governed, and it was not considered odd that a successor to the archbishopric and electorate of Cologne, for example, who was not ordained, should seek a papal dispensation so that he need not take any priestly vows for as long a period as ten years.

Such a far-flung empire inevitably created power struggles, which were complicated by the division of the states into Catholic and Protestant realms, and in fact the greatest threat to the Catholic Hapsburg emperors in Vienna came ultimately from within, in the shape of the rulers of Protestant Brandenburg-Prussia. Indeed it was a struggle that was not finally resolved until the King of Prussia was proclaimed Emperor of Germany at Versailles in 1871, and was then prolonged into the present century and resulted, some would maintain, in two world wars. Be that as it may, what is at once apparent is that before 1871 there was no automatically accepted concept of a German Empire, and even today the concept of Germany differs enormously from place to place. Some see the present partition of the country into East and West as merely a re-affirmation of ancient divisions that supranationalism – in the guise of German imperialism – was unable to overcome.

It is not at all surprising, then, that Ludwig van Beethoven should have looked upon Bonn as his fatherland in the way that he did. The component states of the empire had a very strong conception of their individuality, and their rulers vied with each other to make their own particular courts centres of culture and magnificence according to their means which, in some cases, was remarkably little. The more flamboyant and prosperous rulers could afford to bring famous foreigners to their courts as architects, painters, musicians and writers, and pay to keep them there. Of course this fashion was not only prevalent among the rulers of the imperial states but throughout the whole of Europe. It was simply the custom of the day, and more or less what was expected of any ruler.

Such a widespread feeling of the need to have a brilliant court to prop up one's prestige in the eyes of fellow rulers, or merely to bolster one's self-esteem, resulted in considerable mobility amongst the artistic community; the trend was increased in the wake of dynastic marriages between ruling families, and the fluctuations of the tides of fortune as the relative strengths of opposing factions waxed and waned. To take an example that has a direct bearing on the Beethoven story, Maximilian Emanuel, Elector of Bavaria, took as his second wife a daughter of John Sobieski of Poland. Maximilian was Governor General in Brussels, however, at the time his third son was born on 17 August 1700, and it was this son, Clemens August, who became Elector of Cologne in 1724. Notwithstanding his birth in Brussels, there was already an established connection with the Low Countries, since the Elector

A view of Bonn in the eighteenth century. One sees how small, though elegant, the seat of the electoral government was at this time. Beethoven had a deep affection for it throughout the whole of his life.

In addition to the palace in Bonn, the electors had another residence at Brühl. Although the numbers of musicians in employment varied under successive rulers, there was always an adequate establishment to provide the singers and instrumentalists for both sacred and secular music, and three generations of Beethovens served as court musicians.

of Cologne was also titular Bishop of Liège, and so it is not surprising that we should find a series of Flemish-sounding names among the court musicians.

In 1695, for example, a decree issued at Liège by the previous elector, Joseph Clemens, had appointed Heinrich van den Eeden to the musical establishment, and van den Eedens remained on the payroll until 1782. Gilles van den Eeden was second organist, without salary, at the accession of the new elector, Clemens August, in May 1724, and almost three years later, in February 1727, he was confirmed in his post. One assumes that this can hardly have caused the new elector much heart searching, however, if it was not going to cost him a salary. Even so, van den Eeden must have pleased the authorities with his playing, for early in June of the following year he was granted a salary of 100 florins, and a year later this was increased to 200. The example of Gilles van den Eeden is interesting not only because it illustrates the mobility of artists, and musicians in particular, at this time, but also because of the Flemish connection, and the fact that he was a

colleague of grandfather Ludwig van Beethoven, and possibly one of the first teachers of the young Ludwig.

As to why Bonn was the capital of the electorate, and not the city of Cologne itself, the explanation lay in the nature of the Holy Roman Empire. Cologne was an imperial free city, and its archbishops had no civil or political power within its walls. They might not even stay within the city boundaries for more than three days at a time. For this reason, since the mid-thirteenth century, the rulers had resided in Bonn.

The Beethoven family originally came from the Low Countries, or what is nowadays Belgium. Ludwig's grandfather, also called Ludwig, moved to Bonn as a young man, and in March 1733 he became a bass singer in the court chapel of the Elector of Cologne, who was by that time the Bavarian, Clemens August. Initially the annual salary was 400 florins, and after some thirteen years in the elector's service this was increased by 100 florins on 22 August 1746. His son Johann, who became Beethoven's father, was also on the staff of the musical foundation at Bonn, as we learn from a petition presented to the elector in March 1765 for official recognition of his situation, for he claimed that he had been singing in the court chapel for four years by then. The matter was referred to the Director of the Chamber Music, Gottwald, who endorsed the application (though in so doing conceded only two years' service), and the decree for recognition of Johann as a court musician finally went through on 25 March 1756, when he was sixteen years old.

Elector Clemens August died on 6 February 1761 at Ehrenbreitstein in the palace of the Elector of Trier, where he had stopped on his way to visit his family in Munich. He had arrived on the afternoon of the previous day, was unable to eat dinner, yet threw himself into the subsequent dancing with zest, fainted, and died the next day. So passed away the last of the five Bavarian electors of Cologne. His successor was Maximilian Friedrich of Königsegg-Rothenfels, Count of Königsegg-Aulendorf, who was already Dean of Cologne Cathedral when he was appointed elector on 6 April 1761. Although the new elector eventually enjoyed considerable popularity amongst his people, initially his advent was greeted with a certain amount of resentment when he put a stop to some of the more lavish aspects of his predecessor's tenure of office. In fact a rhyme came into circulation which ran:

> Bei Clemens August trug man blau und weiss,
> Da lebte man wie im Paradeis;
> Bei Max Friedrich trug man sich schwarz und roth,
> Da litt man Hunger wie die schwere Noth.

At Clemens August's we wore blue and white [referring to the colours of Bavaria], then we lived in Paradise; at Max Friedrich's we wore black and red [Max Friedrich was a Swabian], then we endured hunger as in a time of famine.

At all events, we have plenty of witnesses who went to Bonn at this time, such as the Englishman Thomas Pennant, who made his *Tour on the Continent* in 1765, within four years of Max Friedrich's accession, and wrote of it:

> Landed there about seven o'clock. The palace makes a fine figure from the water, having a most extensive front. The town is large, the streets narrow and ill built, the fortifications strong but seem to have been long in a pacific state – the ditches being fruitful gardens and the ramparts covered with vines.
>
> The Elector's palace is adjacent, a very large white pile, seemingly built at several times. The staircase is very handsome, cased with a mock marble and well stuccoed; the ceiling is exceedingly well painted, the subject Phoebus and several of his attendants that are made to float very lightly.

Not long after Max Friedrich's accession, the post of Kapellmeister became vacant, and Ludwig petitioned for it, since he had in any case been carrying out the dual functions of bass singer and Kapellmeister in the interregnum that occurred after the death of a previous incumbent. He hoped to be appointed to the post at that time, but Joseph Touchemoulin or Dousmolin (1727?-1801) had been preferred. Now, however, the economies imposed by the new elector entailed a reduction in salaries, and Touchemoulin decided to resign. In anticipation of the resignation, Beethoven had already been asked to take over once more, and this time he determined to prevent his being passed over yet again. Finally he was given the post, by a decree dated 16 July 1761, and just over a year later his son Johann was officially promised the first vacancy for a court musician that should occur. This happened suddenly in December 1763, when the soprano Madame Lentner left without notice, and Johann and Anna Maria Ries were appointed and paid out of what had been Lentner's salary. Anna Maria was the daughter of another court musician, Johann Ries, and her

The magnificent staircase and main hall at the palace at Brühl.

brother Franz and his son Ferdinand were to play a large part in the story of Ludwig van Beethoven's life, as we shall see later.

As an indication of what sort of activities the court musicians were involved in at this time, the celebrations for the birthday of the elector on 13 May each year were especially important. On that day in 1767, for example, festivities began with a cannon salute from the city walls, after which the court and people were permitted to kiss the electoral hand. There then followed a solemn High Mass accompanied by more artillery. Dinner, to which the papal nuncio, the foreign diplomats and nobility were invited, was taken in public, accompanied by more music and followed by an assembly, for which a serenata was specially composed. There was also a comic opera in the court theatre, with Johann van Beethoven singing the part of Dorindo in *La Schiava Finta*, probably by Piccini. Supper for 130 guests was followed by a masked ball which went on until 5 a.m.

Christmas always was, and still is, a busy time for Church musicians, and eighteenth-century Bonn was no exception. The Midnight Mass in the court chapel was a particularly important event, since the celebrant was the elector himself in his capacity as Archbishop of Cologne. All the nobility and household attended in state, and the electoral bodyguard in full dress uniform lined the chapel. Outside, a complete regiment lined the route from the Koblenzertor to the chapel, and they fired three volleys after the first Gospel, half-way through the Mass, and after the last Gospel, echoed by cannon from the city walls.

The gala dress of the court musicians was particularly splendid. It consisted of green coat, green buckled knee breeches, white or black silk stockings and shoes with black bows. The waistcoat was of white flowered silk, bordered with a cord of gold thread. The musicians' hair was dressed with curls and a pigtail, and the uniform was completed with cocked hat and sword with a silver sword belt. Since it was often cold at Christmas when the Beethoven family and their friends returned home, they ate broiled sausages and drank hot wine, punch and coffee. On such occasions all would usually be good humour and jollity, but it was not always so.

At times grandfather Ludwig had difficulty in imposing his will on the chapel choir—a situation by no means unusual—and he was obliged to resort to an official directive from the elector himself to back up his authority (26 April 1768). We also find from a petition in the archives dated 17 November 1769, that Johann had difficulty living on his salary of 100 florins, and on the death of a colleague, Haveck, hoped to have his salary doubled. In the event he only managed to extract an extra twenty-five florins. Johann had been the only one of grandfather Ludwig's three children to

Christoph Willibald Gluck (1714-87). One of his pupils was Salieri, who taught Beethoven Italian vocal writing. Gluck's patrons were the Lobkowitz family, whose generosity Beethoven also enjoyed.

survive, but from Johann's marriage to Maria Magdalena Keverich seven children resulted. Only three of those seven survived infancy, but even three children require food and clothing, and this factor may well explain Johann's apparently constant eye to increasing his income.

It was about this time, then, that Ludwig was born. We do not know exactly when, but he was baptised in Bonn on 17 December 1770. The date of his birth has usually been taken to have occurred two days previously, on 15 December, and certainly he seems to have regarded that date as his birthday, though there was a tradition in Bonn, and the Catholic Rhineland generally, not to allow more than twenty-four hours to elapse between birth and baptism, so that 16 December would seem more probable. The two remaining brothers were Caspar Anton Carl, baptised on 8 April 1774, and Nikolaus Johann, baptised on 2 October 1776.

Many of the court musicians divided their time between church music and the theatre, partly because of financial considerations but also, we may assume, simply because they enjoyed it. Grandfather Ludwig and Johann appeared on stage as father and son in 1771 in a piece by Grétry, and in 1773 Ludwig even appeared on stage in the last year of his life, when he sang the part of Brunoro in a work by Lucchesi mounted for the elector's birthday, which was celebrated that year on 30 May. However, he must already have been showing signs of fatigue, for on 23 January that year Joseph Demmer had petitioned the elector for the old man's job. In the event grandfather Ludwig died on 24 December 1773, and although his grandson was barely three years old at the time, young Ludwig admired him all his life, and kept his portrait with him in Vienna when he settled there.

At the time of grandfather Ludwig's death, his wife was either living in an ecclesiastical establishment in Cologne (Köln), or simply the Kölnstrasse in Bonn. It is not clear how long she had been there, but what is certain is that she had taken to drink. They had married relatively young – he was twenty and she nineteen – and life cannot have been easy for her. The pair had their way to make, and what was probably the depressive effect of the death of her other children must not be underestimated. There is a tradition that old Ludwig also dealt in wine, in addition to his musical activities, and this may have proved too strong a temptation for his wife, as it did later for his son Johann.

As a family the Beethovens seemed destined to experience unhappiness through marital situations, for Ludwig disapproved of the choice of a partner made by his son Johann, and possibly – if not probably – for this reason father and son had separate homes. Subsequently young Ludwig was to disapprove violently of his brothers' choice of wives. This unhappiness through matrimony must not be forgotten in view of its potential effect upon the young Ludwig in his relationships with women later in life, and especially in his dealings with his nephew Karl. He expended an enormous amount of energy in trying to put Karl out of reach of what he regarded as the bad influence of the boy's mother. This is by no means to suggest that Beethoven disliked women altogether. He became very attached to a number of women in the course of his life, and he always regretted the fact that he had no wife of his own. Even so, it was a particularly difficult area for him, and had some deep psychological implications, as we shall see later.

Ludwig's mother married the valet of the Elector of Trier at the age of sixteen, but found herself a widow before she was nineteen. It seems that the only possible reason that grandfather Ludwig could have had for opposing the wedding, namely that Johann's chosen bride was his social inferior, turned out to be of no account, for she proved to be a very serious-minded and capable person, and young Ludwig came to refer to her in after years as an excellent mother. Johann, too,

seems to have held her in affection, as we learn from the Fischer manuscript, and every year on her birthday and saint's day (both fell on 22 July), she would retire to bed early, then be awakened by music which her husband organised. She dressed and attended the recital, which was followed by food and drink and dancing.

One must treat the Fischer manuscript with a certain amount of reserve, but it is important for the light it throws on the composer's early years in Bonn. Although young Ludwig was born in the Bonngasse, by the time he was five or six the family had moved first into the Dreieckplatz, and then into the Fischer house in the Rheingasse. They were living there when Gottfried Fischer, ten years younger than Ludwig, was born. The Fischer manuscript, then, consists of Gottfried's reminiscences, together with those of his sister Cäcilie, who was some eight years older than Ludwig, but who survived to the age of eighty-five and died on 23 May 1845. Gottfried died in 1864. When the Beethoven monument was unveiled in Bonn in 1838, the Fischers were still living in the Rheingasse, and many visitors went to see them, and so inspired the writing of the manuscript. Gottfried went on adding to it until 1857, but whereas his sister remained alert and mentally active to the end of her life, he became somewhat senile. Moreover he had little or no formal education as a child, hence the reason for treating his manuscript with reservations.

The Beethovens moved from the Rheingasse to the Neugasse – according to the Fischers – in the course of 1776. This new address was supposed to have the advantage of being closer to the market, the church and the electoral palace, though Johann seems to have found it rather gloomy, since it looked out on to the wall of the Franciscan monastery. As it happened, the decision to move yet again was more or less made for him, when a serious fire ravaged the palace in 1777. Since the Fischer apartment was still available, back the Beethovens went. So many removals early in Ludwig's life may well help to explain why he became so peripatetic later, when he lived in Vienna.

We are told in the Fischer manuscript that Ludwig went first to an elementary school in the Neugasse, and then to the school attached to Bonn Cathedral. Subsequently he went to a school in the Bonngasse, but it seems unlikely that he went on to the gymnasium or high school. We are probably safe in assuming that by that time it was obvious that his musical talent was what really mattered most, though as to how or when Ludwig's musical gifts were first manifest we have little or no information. This has led to a wide variety of somewhat romantic pictures, ranging from that of the prodigy delighted to be put on his father's knee so as to be able to reach the piano keyboard with his tiny fingers, to the complete opposite of a tyrannical father forcing his child to practise for hours on end, and even on occasion locking him in the cellar. Fischer's vivid recollection that has come down to us of seeing the tiny Ludwig standing on a stool in front of the piano was subsequently corroborated from other sources, so this at least was not simply part of the romantic picture.

As ever, the truth probably lay somewhere between the two. It seems unlikely, to start with, that Ludwig was a child prodigy on the lines of Handel, Haydn or Mozart. Nevertheless he obviously gave some early signs of talent, and his father determined to produce that talent to the full. He gave his son lessons for the piano and violin, and possibly also viola. What is much more doubtful, however, is whether one may jump from that to the assumption that Johann was determined to exploit his son's talent to the full financially. Certainly the family finances were in a bad way, and they probably got worse in direct proportion to the increase in Johann's drinking habits. History has painted him as a scheming, avaricious father who cared nothing for his son's career than that he should make money. Whilst still allowing that this may have been so, one must also admit that other elements were probably present.

L. Radoux's portrait of Ludwig van Beethoven (1712-73), the composer's grandfather, to whom he remained attached all his life. Old Ludwig was born in Antwerp, but moved to Bonn, where he eventually became Kapellmeister at the electoral court, and so founded the Beethoven musical dynasty there.

It may have been avarice, then, or misguided business sense, or merely paternal pride, that induced Johann to advertise his son's age as a year less than it actually was, when he made his first public appearance in Bonn: 'This day, 26 March 1778, in the music concert room in the Sternengasse, the Electoral Court Tenor, Beethoven, will have the honour of presenting two of his pupils, namely Mlle Averdonc, Court Contralto, and his young son aged six. The first will have the honour of contributing various fine arias, and the second various piano concertos and trios . . .' Whatever Johann's motives, however, we have no record that the concert was either a financial or an artistic success. What it seems to have achieved, however, was to make Johann realise that his instruction was no longer adequate for his son, and that he would have to look farther afield. In view of the development of Ludwig's talent, therefore, posterity ought to be grateful that the concert was not a great success, for without it he may have been left solely to his father's tuition, and his career might never have developed in the way it did.

Initially Johann turned for help to his immediate musical colleagues. It is possible that for the piano he went first to the court organist Gilles van den Eeden, whom we have already met, but he was by now a very old man, having come to Bonn before Ludwig's grandfather, and in any case he does not seem to have made much impression on the boy. There was also Tobias Friedrich Pfeiffer, a tenor who was in Bonn during 1779 for the theatrical season, and a friend of Ludwig's father, who also gave him some piano lessons, but on a very irregular basis. Tradition has it that on some occasions when Pfeiffer and Johann van Beethoven came home from their drinking nights late, Ludwig would be roused from his bed and kept at the keyboard until the morning. Then there was the violinist Franz Georg Rovantini, who lived in the Fischer house, too. He gave Ludwig lessons on the violin and the viola, but they came to an abrupt end when Rovantini died at the early age of twenty-four on 9 September 1781. Franz Ries also gave the boy violin lessons. Two more early teachers were those for the organ, namely a Franciscan friar, Willibald Koch, and Zenser, the organist of Bonn Cathedral.

All of these were of much less importance, however, than Christian Gottlob Neefe (1748-1798), who came to Bonn in 1779 with Grossmann's theatrical company – the same company as the tenor Pfeiffer – but settled there, and in February 1781 was appointed court organist. As an example of how frequently one encounters contradictions in accounts of the early part of Beethoven's life, there is a passage in the *Biographische Notizien über Beethoven*, published by Franz Gerhard Wegeler and Ferdinand Ries in 1838, in which Wegeler affirmed that Neefe had little influence on the education

*Johann van Beethoven (1740-92), the composer's
father, in an engraving by K. B. Beckenkamp.
Probably less talented than his father, and certainly
less so than his son, Johann was nevertheless steeped
in the traditions of court music at Bonn. His somewhat
ill-fated attempt to turn young Ludwig into a child
prodigy had, eventually, the beneficial effect of sending
the boy to more competent teachers.*

*Maria Magdalena Keverich, Beethoven's mother,
who died in 1787. The composer was extremely fond
of his long-suffering mother, and her death came as a
great blow to him. Beckenkamp's engraved portrait
suggests something of the mark life made on her, not
least through a drunken and unreliable husband.*

of the young Ludwig, and that the latter complained that Neefe was much too critical of his early attempts at composition. We have, however, a letter to Neefe from Ludwig himself—one of the earliest that has come down to us—in which he states quite clearly: 'Thank you for the advice you have so often given me about progress in my God-given art. If ever I become a great man, you also will have shared in my success . . .'

From Neefe's own side there can be little doubt of his view on the matter. He contributed to Cramer's *Magazin der Musik* of 2 March 1783 what turned out to be a prophetic utterance:

> Louis van Beethoven, son of the tenor . . . a boy of eleven years of age and of very promising talent. He plays the clavier with much skill and force, sight reads very well and—to put it in a nutshell—he plays above all 'The Well-Tempered Clavichord' of Sebastian Bach, which Herr Neefe put into his hands.

Those who know this collection of preludes and fugues in every key—which might almost be termed the *non plus ultra* of our art—will appreciate what this means. As far as his duties permitted, Herr Neefe has also given him tuition in through bass. He is now teaching him composition, and so as to encourage him has had nine variations for the pianoforte, written by him on a march [by Ernst Christoph Dressler], engraved at Mannheim. This young genius deserves help to enable him to travel. He would certainly become a second Wolfgang Amadeus Mozart if he were to continue as he has begun.

Within four years the two composers—Beethoven and Mozart—were to meet in Vienna, and when the latter heard Beethoven's playing he is reported to have said: 'Keep your eyes on him; some day he will give the world something to talk about.'

*The memorial room in the Beethovenhaus, with the
marble bust by Wolff-Voss.*

In fact Wegeler's account of Beethoven's relationship with Neefe is not all that contradictory when one looks at it a little more closely, and especially in view of what Neefe revealed in the previous extract as his predilection for Bach's music. His instruction for the young Ludwig in composition was doubtless strict and traditional in musical terms, whereas Ludwig was already, even in his first compositions, showing signs of originality. There is a story that when he had finished one of his first compositions, a funeral cantata, he presented it to his grandfather's successor as electoral Kapellmeister, Andrea Lucchesi, asking him to correct the faults. Lucchesi returned the score, saying that since he did not understand it, he was unable to correct the errors. Even so, he put on a performance of the work. The performers, when confronted by the music at the first rehearsal, evinced 'great astonishment at the originality of the composition'—which must surely be one of the greatest musical understatements of the day, though after a few rehearsals they evidently grew to like the work, and it was received well at its first performance.

Although strict rules of harmony and counterpoint may have a detrimental effect in some cases when students are grappling with early composition exercises, this tends to be the exception rather than the rule, and it is easier for a composer to know himself fully and evolve his own musical language when he is first the complete master of the structural elements of his craft. If Neefe was perhaps a little too keen on Bach's music where his pupil was concerned, then he could hardly have chosen a better composer as an example. Moreover it was a particularly enlightened choice. Much of Bach's music went out of favour after his death, and even in his own lifetime his sons had found him old-fashioned. The Bach 'revival' did not get under way until considerably later. In the circumstances, therefore, Neefe was doing Ludwig a great favour. He also had sufficient confidence in his pupil's ability to leave him in charge as organist when he went away in June 1782, and during the ensuing theatre season of 1782-83 Ludwig took on the exacting task of playing the pianoforte or harpsichord in the orchestra.

At the age of twelve, therefore, he began to gain the experience in sight reading and the ability to play from complicated scores that made people marvel so in later years, and he also heard the current repertoire of German, Italian and French opera. Had things continued

*Beethoven's birthplace in Bonn. This, and the
adjoining building, now house the Beethoven Archive.*

Above: The organ in the Minorite Monastery in Bonn. Beethoven played it at the age of nine, substituting for the monastery organist.

Below: The room in which Beethoven was born.

in this way at Bonn, Beethoven might well have become a fluent, if not prolific, composer of operas. One cannot help but feel, however, that so much exposure to rather facile and shallow operatic music in these early years helped to form his determination to go deeper in his own music. By now he had published music of his own; the Dressler variations already mentioned, and three sonatas which appeared in 1783, and which he dedicated to the Elector Maximilian Friedrich. His age, incidentally, was still given on the title page as a year younger than it was, i.e. eleven instead of twelve. Then on the last day of February of the next year, 1784, he was officially confirmed as Neefe's assistant in the electoral chapel. Normally this would simply have served to strengthen his foothold on the ladder of a worthy career in the old tradition of court music, but events took a dramatic turn and Elector Maximilian Friedrich died on 15 April. The situation altered overnight. The theatre season was abandoned and the company disbanded with a month's pay. Kapellmeister Lucchesi returned to Bonn, and there was no longer any call for the services of a second organist. Luckily, however, the necessary documents had been completed by the time the list of current members of the musical foundation was drawn up for the new elector, and Ludwig's name was included.

Maximilian Friedrich's successor was a Hapsburg archduke, Maximilian Franz, and son of no less a personage than the Empress Maria-Theresa herself. The succession was by no means unexpected, however, and had been prepared well in advance. The Austrian Chancellor, Prince Kaunitz, was attempting to counter Prussian influence within the Holy Roman Empire. It was obvious that Maximilian Friedrich had no heir and would not live much longer, so on 7 August 1780 Maria-Theresa's youngest son Maximilian Franz was elected coadjutor to the Elector of Cologne, and on 16th of the same month coadjutor to one of the other sees held in plurality, that of Münster.

The new elector had initially followed a military career, and taken part in the Bavarian campaign with his brother Joseph, but fell from his horse in 1778, and so abandoned the army for the Church. Mozart, writing to his father on 17 November 1781, was suitably wry about this transformation:

> When God gives a man office he also gives him understanding. This is really what has happened with the archduke. Before he became a priest he was much wittier and more clever and talked less but more sensibly. You should see him now! Stupidity looks out through his eyes, he talks unceasingly, always in falsetto; his throat is swollen. In a word, the man has been completely transformed.

But as Maximilian Franz took his new possessions in

hand, he proved to be a much more conscientious and inspiring ruler than Mozart's opinion would have allowed for. For example, he ignored the papal dispensation from making his priestly vows for a period of ten years, obtained for him by his mother, and duly entered the seminary in Cologne–even if he did manage to complete all the necessary formalities in the space of three weeks. He also pressed for the granting of a university to Bonn from his brother the Emperor Joseph (as he now was since the death of Maria-Theresa), though this had in fact been set on foot by his predecessor as elector. What was more important was the atmosphere that he generated in Bonn. It was still a small place in those days–not more than 8,000 or 9,000 inhabitants–so that it was therefore easy for a person in such a prominent position to make his presence and personality widely felt. This was the atmosphere in which Ludwig van Beethoven began to grow up, and in later years Franz Gerhard Wegeler, looking back on that time, was to say: '. . . it was a fine and in

many ways exciting time in Bonn so long as it was ruled by the genial elector Max Franz, Maria-Theresa's youngest and favourite son.'

Even so, his period of rule began with a thorough enquiry into the entire administration and household, which must have revived memories of the contrast between the last years of Clemens August and the advent of Maximilian Friedrich. In a document of 25 June 1784, Johann van Beethoven was declared to be of little further use as a singer, and very poor–though it was also noted that he was of long-standing service, married, and of good conduct. Neefe, too, was rather dismissed as being of little worth, and in his case he also had against him the fact that he was a Protestant to

The advertisement for Ludwig van Beethoven's first public appearance, as a child prodigy, in Bonn in 1778. In order to make the child seem even more of a prodigy, his father deliberately falsified his age, and made him a year younger than he actually was.

boot. Ludwig was the only one who received anything approaching approval, and we learn that although his appointment as assistant organist was regarded as beyond question, he had not so far received any salary. A further document suggested that Neefe might very well be removed and the young Beethoven appointed in his place. This would mean a considerable saving on salaries, since Ludwig might be had, in the opinion of the compiler of the report, for 150 florins.

In the event the attempt to oust Neefe failed, though his salary was reduced to 200 florins, which induced him to start looking round for new employment. Happily the new elector seems to have come to a more favourable estimate of Neefe's worth, however, for on 8 February 1785 his old salary was restored to him. That year Johann van Beethoven received 200 florins, and Ludwig 100.

The same year, 1785, saw the composition of three piano quartets, WoO. 36 (WoO. stands for Work without Opus number), which were never published during the composer's lifetime, though he used elements from them in other works. They do not bear comparison with the piano quartets written at a comparable age by Mendelssohn, but then one must remember that such a combination of instruments—piano, violin, viola and

C. G. Neefe (1748-98) in a portrait by Rosenberg engraved by Liebe. He was quick to recognise Beethoven's talent and ensured that he was given every encouragement for its development.

cello—was virtually unknown at the time. Of course these are more in the way of being piano sonatas with strings than what is commonly thought of as true piano quartets; even so, Beethoven's piano quartets are even earlier than those of Mozart, in which case he had nothing at all to use as a model. Naturally there was other music written in this period, but it was becoming increasingly obvious that Ludwig needed more than Bonn could provide in the way of musical tuition and ambiance.

The last of the Beethoven children, a girl, was born early in May 1786, but she lived little more than a year. For young Ludwig, life might have seemed to have settled down into a routine, and yet as early as 1783 Neefe had said that Ludwig deserved support in order to travel. Four years later it had become even more imperative. Bonn may very well have been, in the words of a writer in Cramer's *Magazin der Musik* dated 8 April 1787: '. . . becoming more and more attractive for music-lovers through the gracious patronage of our beloved elector . . .' but it was nevertheless only a provincial city when compared with London, Paris or Vienna, and it was to this last city that Beethoven now made his way.

Unfortunately the official records in Düsseldorf are incomplete at this point, so there is no trace of any application for leave from Ludwig. He seems to have continued to draw his salary, however, so one may assume that his absence was officially approved. This money alone, however, would hardly have been sufficient to finance a trip to Vienna, and it is very tempting to speculate as to how he was able to afford it. It is often assumed that the elector helped, and this cannot be ruled out, but there is no proof that he did so at this stage. In fact the evidence clearly indicates that Ludwig hardly had sufficient money for the barest necessities, and was obliged to borrow some in Augsburg on the return journey. Of course if he had envisaged a longish stay in Vienna, then he might have hoped to find employment, or make money from giving lessons, and the fact that he was obliged to return to Bonn fairly quickly, because of his mother's failing health, upset his plans on this score.

Be that as it may, he achieved his chief objective in Vienna, which was to meet Mozart and have lessons from him. Unfortunately the period from 7 April to 20 April 1787, when Beethoven most likely seems to have been in Vienna, cannot have been the best time for contacting Mozart. His father died on 28 May that year, and he was busy with the composition of *Don Giovanni*. His initial lack of interest in Beethoven may well have been merely preoccupation, then, coupled with the fact that although Beethoven performed well for him, his standards were naturally very high, and Mozart would automatically have assumed that the young Beethoven would have worked up one or two audition pieces which he ought, therefore, to have played well in any circumstances. It was only when Mozart gave Beethoven a theme on which to improvise that the former became aware of the great talent of the latter. We have already seen what Mozart's opinion of the young Beethoven was on that occasion, and it must be a cause for regret that the period of contact was not more intensive. Beethoven never achieved facility in his composition, and all his life had to work hard at his creations. Help from Mozart on this point might well have eased the exhausting process of giving expression to the musical thoughts in his mind.

As to the dates for the trip, one can only give the probable ones. There was a tradition that Beethoven was only impressed by two people on that first visit to Vienna, namely Mozart and the Emperor Joseph. We know that Joseph was absent from Vienna between 11 April and 30 June on a visit to the Crimea with the Russian Empress Catherine. Beethoven passed through Munich on 1 April, so had probably left Bonn on 20 March, and arrived in Vienna on 7 April, not long before Emperor Joseph's departure. He returned via Munich on 25 April, so must have left Vienna on 20 April or thereabouts. One must be wary of laying too much stress on the person of the emperor as a determining factor in the chronology, however, for though it is by no means impossible that the young composer should have had a personal audience with the emperor in this period, especially since he was in the employ of his brother, Elector Maximilian Franz, we must also allow that there must have been many other, more important, matters requiring the emperor's attention before his departure. However, Beethoven may well have seen him in public, or even been present in the same room as the emperor. Although Beethoven was never one to be unduly impressed with people of high rank *per se*, one does not encounter emperors every day, and he may well have been impressed by Joseph at a distance. If the young Beethoven had been hoping for some court appointment, then it must have been doubly frustrating, having come so close to the emperor, to have to leave Vienna so soon.

The final words on the matter are best left to Ludwig himself, in the letter from Bonn, dated 15 September 1787, which he wrote to Dr Schaden, the lawyer who loaned him money in Augsburg:

> I can easily imagine what you must think of me, and I cannot deny that you have good reasons for not thinking favourably of me. However, I shall not attempt to justify myself until I explain why I hope that my apologies will be accepted. I have to tell you that as soon as I left Augsburg my cheerfulness and my health, too, began to decline. The nearer

Maximilian Franz, Archduke of Austria and Elector of Cologne, in an engraving dating from 1782. It was during his period of office that Beethoven first went to Vienna to seek out Mozart, and the Elector may have provided financial assistance.

> I got to my native city the more frequent became my father's letters urging me to travel as fast as possible, because my mother was not in a good state of health. Consequently I travelled as quickly as I could, especially since I began to feel ill myself. My desire to see my dying mother once more overcame all obstacles for me, and helped me to surmount the greatest difficulties. I found my mother still alive, but in the most terrible state. She was suffering from consumption, and she finally died about seven weeks ago after a great deal of pain and agony. She was such a good, loving mother to me, and my best friend.

Ludwig then went on to reveal that he had been suffering from asthma continually since his return to Bonn, and he was afraid that it would turn into the consumption that had carried off his mother. He had also had

*Vienna in Mozart's time. An engraving of the
Imperial War Chancery and the Garrison Church
in 1780 by C. Schütz.*

deep fits of melancholy, which he found almost as bad as the illness itself. Indeed, today one would be inclined to say that his whole condition was largely psychosomatic, and illness – whether real or imaginary – is a recurrent theme of the letters throughout Beethoven's life. He then went on to refer to the three carolins or gold coins that Schaden had loaned him in Augsburg, but indicated that he was as yet unable to repay them, since the journey had been expensive, and prospects were looking far from good in Bonn. As he said himself, Fate was not being very kind to him.

Despite indications of financial help from Franz Ries, conditions were actually much worse in Bonn than Ludwig indicated in his letter, especially within the Beethoven family. His father had been driven to such extremes through his wife's prolonged illness that he had to sell some of his possessions and pawn others. He therefore petitioned the elector on 24 July for an advance of 100 florins on his salary. Although there is no official record of it, there must also have been the problem of his father's drinking, too. Fate had yet one more blow to deliver, however, for on 25 November the little baby Margaretha died, and as his seventeenth birthday approached and the year ended, there can

have been little for Ludwig to look forward to. His brief moment of escape to Vienna must have seemed like the passage of a dragonfly across a bed of water-lilies, and about as transitory. In such circumstances things simply had to get better, for they could hardly have been worse.

Ludwig still had his post as organist, however, as well as his post as viola player in the court orchestra, and in the course of 1788 the elector began to assemble a theatrical company for the winter season. Ludwig was engaged as viola player, and the experience of the two orchestras can only have been beneficial both from a financial and a musical point of view, for it gave him invaluable insight into the business of orchestration.

The first season opened on 3 January 1789, and lasted until 23 May. A second season opened on 13 October 1789 and lasted through into the next year, but was interrupted for a space on 24 February 1790 when news reached Bonn of the death of Emperor Joseph, who was the Elector Maximilian's brother. By the time the third season began, on 23 October 1790, Ludwig seems to have managed to recoup the finances of the family somewhat, and it had been officially agreed by a decree dated 20 November 1789 that his father's services would be dispensed with; but his

20

salary would continue to be paid, though he would only receive half of it, and the other half would be paid to Ludwig.

By now Ludwig had made friends with two families who were to be of immense help to him, not only through their wealth and influence, but because they gave him access to a totally different ambiance where culture and refinement were deeply rooted, and the creative and artistic processes admired. The first of these was the von Breuning family whose head, Emanuel Joseph, was a court councillor until his death in the palace fire of 1777. His son Stephan was a close friend of Ludwig. The second family was the Waldsteins, and its head, Ferdinand Ernst Gabriel, Count von Waldstein, was to become a close friend of the elector. For the theatrical season mentioned above, Ludwig wrote and had performed a *Ritterballet* on 6 March 1791, just two days before the conclusion of the season. In one of the reports of the event it is revealed that the theme of the ballet, which was performed by the nobility in old German costume, was war, the chase, love and drinking. Both the conception and the music were attributed to Count Waldstein, but the music was by Ludwig van Beethoven. This testifies to the regard in which, by this time, Count Waldstein held Ludwig, for it was a demonstration of his confidence in him that he asked the young composer to write the music, and the closeness of their working relationship. One might have hoped that it would have been made apparent sooner, and more readily, who the real composer was.

However, Christmas 1790 had seen a visitor to Bonn who was to rekindle all the old yearning in Ludwig's heart for a more stimulating environment and broader musical influences. Joseph Haydn, on his way to London with Johann Peter Salomon, attended Mass in the electoral chapel on the Sunday after Christmas, heard a performance of one of his own works, and afterwards was presented to each of the virtuosi in turn by the elector himself. We do not know what conversation, if any, passed between Haydn and the young Beethoven, but we do know that on the return journey from London Haydn again passed through Bonn, in July 1792, and

The young Beethoven–he was not quite seventeen–playing for Mozart in Vienna in 1787. The painting by Hugues Merle is rather fanciful in its account of the occasion but it is true that Mozart was very impressed by Beethoven.

on this occasion the orchestra gave him breakfast at Godesberg. Beethoven took the opportunity to show the master a cantata he had composed, and the master encouraged him to continue his studies. It may well have been decided there and then that Beethoven would go to Vienna to study with Haydn, and in normal circumstances he would have left Bonn with the master. However, the elector had to give his consent, and he was absent in Frankfurt for the coronation of his nephew Emperor Franz (who succeeded Leopold II – who was the successor of Joseph: just over two years saw three emperors), which took place on 14 July 1792.

During Haydn's time in England Ludwig had been playing in yet another theatrical season in Bonn, this time lasting from 28 December 1791 until 20 February 1792, and a fifth season was to begin in October 1792. However, Ludwig's involvement was to be of short duration, for already during that month he was planning to leave Bonn for Vienna, and 1 November was destined to be the last day he spent in the city, though he did not know that at the time. Initially he had only intended spending a limited period of time in Vienna, but events dictated otherwise, not least the approach of the French revolutionary armies. On 22 October they entered Mainz, and on 24 and 25 October the court archives and treasury were transferred down the Rhine to Düsseldorf.

It was assumed that the elector had helped finance Beethoven's journey to Vienna, and certainly Neefe, writing in the *Berliner Musik-Zeitung* the following year, reported: 'In November of last year Ludwig van Beethoven, assistant court organist and undoubtedly now one of the foremost pianoforte players, went to Vienna at the expense of our elector to Haydn in order to perfect himself under his direction more fully in the art of composition'. In the circumstances, then, certain commentators were led to accuse Beethoven of ingratitude to the elector who had so generously supported him. From Beethoven's side of the affair, however, it all must have seemed horribly like what had happened the last

Panorama of Vienna c. 1775-79 by C. Schütz.
The sheer size and magnificence of Vienna, when compared with provincial Bonn, must have been almost overwhelming for young Beethoven when he paid his first visit to the capital.

time he had set out for Vienna. It certainly seems to have been the elector's intention to increase Beethoven's salary to 600 florins, or 100 ducats, but because of the war and the upheaval it caused, Ludwig only received payment for one quarter—i.e. twenty-five ducats—at this new rate, soon after setting off for Vienna.

To mark his departure from Bonn, several friends wrote inscriptions in an album for him. That of Eleonore von Breuning, Stephan's sister, runs: 'Friendship, together with what is good, grows like the evening shadow until the setting of the sun of life'. In her case, that was to prove to be a particularly appropriate sentiment since, after a long period of apparent silence, she and her husband came into contact with Beethoven towards the end of his life, and brought back happy memories of his early years in Bonn. Count Waldstein's inscription in the album is dated 29 October, and is more prophetic in tone:

> Dear Beethoven. You are going to Vienna in fulfilment of your long-frustrated wishes. Mozart's genius is mourning and weeping

Ferdinand, Count von Waldstein (1762-1823), who was one of those in Bonn who encouraged Ludwig to write music—in particular the Ritterballet of 1791—and to contemplate a return to Vienna. Waldstein was well placed to help the young Beethoven, and had confidence in his talent.

over the death of her pupil [he had died the previous year]. She found a refuge but no occupation with the untiring Haydn; through him she wishes to form a union with another. With the help of hard work you will receive Mozart's spirit at Haydn's hands. Your true friend, Waldstein.

The departure for Vienna is an appropriate point at which to consider what music Ludwig had written up until this point. We have already encountered the Dressler variations, WoO. 63, of 1782; the three piano sonatas, WoO. 47, of 1783; the three piano quartets, WoO. 36, of 1785; and the *Ritterballet* of 1790-91. There were also two cantatas which were not published by Beethoven, one on the death of Joseph II, written between March and June 1790, and the second on the elevation of Leopold II who succeeded him. He was elected Holy Roman Emperor on 30 September and crowned on 9 October 1790. Joseph, Leopold and Elector Maximilian Franz were all children of Maria-Theresa, and therefore brothers, incidentally, of the unfortunate Marie-Antoinette. When Brahms played through the score of the funeral cantata (which may not have been performed partly because of the difficulty of the writing for the wind instruments), he is reported to have said: 'It is Beethoven through and through. Even if there were no name on the title page, it would be impossible to envisage any other than that of Beethoven.'

There were several songs produced during the pre-Vienna period, too, but more important was a concerto for piano in E flat, WoO. 4, dating from 1784, of which only the solo part, with reduction of the orchestral tuttis, survives; a trio in G for piano, flute and bassoon, WoO. 37; a fragment of a concerto in C for violin, WoO. 5, dating from the early 1790s; eight variations in C for piano duet on a theme by Count Waldstein, WoO. 67, composed in 1791-92 and published by Simrock in Bonn in 1794; and the wind octet, published posthumously as Op. 103, though probably composed in 1792, as well as the trio in E flat, Op. 3, for violin, viola and cello, dating from the same year. What is important about these works in relation to Beethoven's career and subsequent development is not their relative merit or worth in critical terms, but that they point the way to what was to unfold in the next phase in Vienna. For one must not forget that initially Beethoven's fame rested largely on his skill as a pianist, and when he arrived in Vienna it was as a pianist that he first became known. He was especially famed for his extemporised improvisations on given themes, which were very popular at the time, and more or less expected as part of the stock in trade of any self-respecting virtuoso – if something that is extemporary can rightly be regarded as 'stock-in-trade'. The point is that the ability to extemporise at the keyboard does not necessarily indicate any great skill at composition, however, since quite a wide range of elements may be employed for effect without there being any cohesive compositional structure to the whole. Indeed, were that so, then the player's performance would cease to be either improvised or extemporary in the strictest sense of the words. What is also true, however, is that in music – as in all the arts – it is impossible to draw up rigidly controlled categories, whereby a person will say: 'I do this and nothing else.' Music has a habit of spilling over at times, and leading its exponents into paths that they might not have envisaged. Sometimes those paths lead nowhere, and one has to turn back, but music would be considerably the poorer if this never happened.

Ultimately it is a question of the performer or composer getting to know himself – his strengths as well as his limitations – and only by taking action will he ever achieve this. In 1792 this is exactly what Ludwig van Beethoven was doing when he set out for Vienna.

Vienna 1792

BEETHOVEN arrived in Vienna on or before 10 November 1792, according to a memorandum book he kept at the time, in which he included the expenses of his journey, and at first—as one might well expect—his arrival caused no great stir. There were, after all, plenty of musicians in the public eye in Vienna in the last decade of the eighteenth century. We may assume that Beethoven contacted Haydn as soon as possible, but he had hardly had time to settle down when news reached him from Bonn that his father had died on 18 December. The event is reputed to have drawn the comment from the Elector of Cologne that the revenues from the excise on liquor had suffered a loss from the death of Beethoven. The pecuniary loss to his son was greater.

Luckily Franz Ries acted for Ludwig back in Bonn, and drew his salary for him, but the situation was serious. Not only had Ludwig been disappointed in his hopes of the 100 ducats, but his father's death meant the immediate end of his pension of 200 florins. Since half the pension had been assigned to Ludwig in any case, we may assume that he and Ries were in correspondence as to how to ensure that it continue to be paid, or replaced. Ludwig wrote to the elector from Vienna, probably at the end of April or early in May 1793, and his request for continuance of the payments was granted by a decree dated 3 May. The order was put through to the exchequer three weeks later, and on 15 June Franz Ries was able to sign for the appropriate sums of money for the first two quarters of the year. Ludwig had been granted 100 florins from his father's pension, in addition to the 100 he was already receiving.

Ludwig was obviously in need of money at this time, but the signs were that as the year progressed the situation began to improve. In July, for example, Artaria published his twelve variations for piano and violin on Mozart's *Se vuol ballare* from *The Marriage of Figaro*, WoO 40, which the composer dedicated to Eleonore von Breuning. The letter listing the necessary corrections is still in existence, written from somewhere 'in the country' in August 1793. It is quite possible that Beethoven had gone to the Esterházy summer residence at Eisenstadt with Haydn, for we have indications from other sources that his contacts with Haydn were not restricted to lessons. The memorandum of expenses contains entries for 24 and 29 October 1793 showing that they had taken chocolate and coffee together, presumably in a cafe. There is also a letter from Haydn to the elector, dated 23 November 1793, sending five works composed by Beethoven, and predicting that on the evidence of these same works it would be quite obvious that one day he would be one of Europe's greatest composers.

Haydn then took the opportunity of informing the elector that he would not be able to continue giving Beethoven lessons, much to his regret (he was getting ready to go to England once more), and he asked the elector to give Beethoven 1,000 florins for the coming year, since Haydn had had to lend him 500 florins out of his own pocket. Beethoven sent a suitably ingratiating letter at the same time, and they awaited the elector's reply. Exactly one month later, on 23 December, the elector retorted that four of the five works sent by Haydn had been composed by Beethoven in Bonn, and that if the young man was simply running into debt, he might as well come home.

By this time there was little more that Haydn could do for his pupil, in view of his impending departure, and the lessons cannot have extended much beyond the end of the year, for on 19 January 1794 Haydn left for England once more. It may well have been his intention to take his pupil with him, but nothing came of it, and Ludwig may not have been sorry, for the lessons with the great man had not been entirely to Beethoven's satisfaction. In fact Beethoven was already receiving some more practical help from the composer Johann Baptist Schenk, and they worked together, virtually behind Haydn's back, with the help of Joseph Fux's textbook *Gradus ad Parnassum*.

Later, after Haydn's departure, Beethoven went to Johann Georg Albrechtsberger for counterpoint, and Antonio Salieri for Italian vocal writing. Beethoven's attitude to his period with Haydn was aptly summed up in his own words in a remark to Ferdinand Ries, to the effect that Haydn had wanted Beethoven to put

'pupil of Haydn' on the title page of his first works. Beethoven's reluctance to do so, he explained, lay in the fact that although he had received some lessons from Haydn, he had never actually learned anything from him. Even so, Beethoven never quarrelled with Haydn, and they remained on good terms.

During this period Beethoven maintained contact with friends in Bonn, despite the fact that he himself admitted that he was not a good correspondent. Letters to Eleonore von Breuning survive, in which there is evidence that he had also written to other friends, and that he still entertained the idea of returning to Bonn in the near future – at least in the earlier letters. Eleonore had made him a waistcoat that he took with him to Vienna, and in his first letter to her after his departure from Bonn he asked her for another one, since the first had gone out of fashion. In those early days he cared about such things. The fact that the letter is dated 2 November 1793, almost a year after his departure, would suggest that it is no wonder the first waistcoat had gone out of fashion. He also told Eleonore in the letter about the piano and violin variations he was dedicating to her (probably WoO. 40), though they

An engraving of Vienna in the early years of the nineteenth century, with the Upper Belvedere in the foreground. The young provincial composer from Bonn found it hard, initially, to make very much impression in the capital. Soon, however, he found noble and princely patrons who accepted his somewhat odd manners because of his supreme musical gift.

had been published some four months before. She did not send him another waistcoat, it would seem, but we have a letter from the following June (1794) in which Beethoven thanks her for a neckcloth she had made for him and sent to him.

Though the tone of these two letters is very affectionate – and there is no reason at all to suppose that it was anything but spontaneous and genuine – Beethoven's feelings towards Eleonore never grew into anything more, since she did not relate to him in that way, and she married Franz Gerhard Wegeler in 1802. In fact Beethoven's position was rather that of an adopted brother, and indeed since the death of his own mother he had tended to look to Madame von Breuning as her replacement. Nevertheless there are indications in the first letter that Beethoven and Eleonore had fallen out or had some misunderstanding which he attributed to the intervention of a third party, and in his first letter to her from Vienna he went to considerable lengths to make sure that all was forgiven and forgotten. Unfortunately these 'misunderstandings' were destined to be a recurring feature of Beethoven's relationships, and cannot have made life easy for his friends.

In 1794 his brother Caspar Anton Carl joined him in Vienna. He brought the news that the Bonn publisher Nikolaus Simrock was intending to engrave the eight variations for piano duet, WoO. 67, without previously having consulted the composer. Naturally Beethoven was worried that what was tantamount to a pirate edition would result, especially if he had in the meantime sold the work to Artaria in Vienna for publication. More important was the fact that he wanted the work to be published as accurately as possible, since in Simrock's edition of his thirteen variations for piano, WoO. 66, the sixth variation had emerged in A major instead of A minor. Beethoven therefore proposed sending the manuscript to Count Waldstein with all his corrections duly incorporated, and Waldstein would then deliver it to Simrock. Eventually Beethoven was more than pleased with the result.

The role played by Caspar Anton Carl in this affair was one that he later took up in earnest, for having hoped to establish himself in Vienna in the same line of business as his brother, in other words as a pianist and composer, he then thought better of it, and in 1800 became a cashier in a state bank. At the same time he acted as Ludwig's go-between with the firm of Breitkopf & Härtel in Leipzig, writing most of the letters to them.

Caspar Anton Carl was not the only person to leave Bonn in 1794. When the Holy Roman Empire declared war on France, the Electorate of Cologne, since it was a German state, could not remain neutral. The French revolutionaries had dethroned Maximilian Franz's sister Marie-Antoinette, and cut off her head, but even so the elector had never had any time for the French

J. B. Schenk (1753-1836), the composer from whom Beethoven received lessons in Vienna in 1793 and 1794, when it became obvious that Haydn's instruction was not to the young composer's taste. Moreover, Haydn's preoccupation with preparations for another visit to London strictly limited the amount of time and attention he was able to devote to Beethoven.

émigrés who crossed the Rhine and caused so much unrest both for the infant French Republic and for the bordering states such as Cologne in which they had taken refuge. In fact Maximilian Franz did his utmost to keep them out of his territories for, he maintained:

> [The] émigré-vermin . . . had either brought on the revolution by their unrestrained, self-seeking, scheming conduct, or else, through their cowardly behaviour, which ran counter to their duty, they had allowed the revolution to gain the upper hand by escaping abroad to posture and swagger as enemies of their fatherland, whereas they should have stayed to expend their property and blood for the sake of preserving a sound order.

Both Maria-Theresa and Joseph had warned Marie-Antoinette well in advance that if she did nothing to try and avert the revolution, then when it came it would be disastrous. They were proved right, but for all his enlightened attitude, Maximilian Franz had to leave

Bonn on 3 October in the face of the French invasion, going first to Frankfurt and then to Münster. Eventually he fixed his residence in Vienna.

Another fugitive from Bonn to Vienna was Franz Gerhard Wegeler. Although only twenty-nine years old, he was already Rector of Bonn University, and may have been a marked man as a result. His account of his arrival in Vienna is useful for the light it throws on the way Beethoven lived then. They had known each other since childhood, and Wegeler had already spent two years in Vienna as a student of medicine. By the time he arrived in October 1794, Beethoven was living as a guest in the house of Prince Karl Lichnowsky, who was a great connoisseur of music and a pianist of no mean accomplishment. He had been both a pupil and a patron of Mozart, and had taken the composer to Prague, Dresden, Leipzig and Berlin in 1789. Obviously by now Beethoven had made his mark in Viennese society, despite his somewhat humble origins.

Prince Lichnowsky held regular music sessions in his house on Friday mornings, when the performers were professional musicians such as Ignaz Schuppanzigh (violin), Franz Weiss (viola), Nicolas Kraft (cello), or the very talented amateur cellist Nikolaus Zmeskall. The sessions were attended by other connoisseurs and musicians, and in such an ambiance it is not surprising that Beethoven soon blossomed, both as far as his music was concerned, and as a personality. Wegeler tells us that Beethoven was always in love at this time, and that he was held in such esteem in the Lichnowsky household that the prince had given orders that if he and Beethoven should ring for a servant at the same time, then Beethoven's wants were to be seen to first. When Beethoven expressed interest in riding on horseback, the prince put his stables at the composer's disposal. For these two reasons, according to Wegeler, Beethoven engaged a servant and bought a horse. However, it would seem that the love of riding did not last long. For one thing, Beethoven was far too preoccupied, most of the time, to think about the poor horse.

Another typical touch is given by Wegeler in relation to Beethoven's eating habits. The prince dined at four, but Beethoven could not bear to come home at half-past three, wash, change and comb his hair, so he often went to taverns where he ate less well and more expensively – much more, since the food at Prince Lichnowsky's was free. No wonder, then, that we have a letter from Beethoven to Zmeskall, probably, dating from this period, asking for the loan of five florins. Generally, however, Lichnowsky must have taken care of Beethoven, and in return Beethoven dedicated several works to him, for example the piano, violin and cello trios of Opus 1. One only hopes that his relationship with his benefactor was always so pleasant. Beet-

hoven easily took offence, or appeared ready to believe the worst of people. One of the enigmas, even shadows, of this period is the existence of a letter to Wegeler which indicates that Beethoven had probably lost his temper and been rude or unkind to Wegeler, and was asking for forgiveness. Apparently much the same thing happened as with Eleonore von Breuning, and when she and Wegeler married, they certainly had that experience with Beethoven in common.

Soon, however, Beethoven was to extend his range in Vienna beyond the musical salons. On 29 and 30 March the annual concerts took place in the Burgtheater for the benefit of the widows' and orphans' fund of the Tonkünstlergesellschaft. On the first evening Beethoven played his piano concerto in B flat, Op. 19, and on the second he improvised at the piano. The next day Beethoven again appeared in public, this time also in the Burgtheater, where Mozart's widow had arranged a performance of *La Clemenza di Tito*. After the first act of the opera Beethoven played a Mozart piano concerto.

As a further testimony to Beethoven's increasing reputation, on 16 May an advertisement appeared inviting subscriptions to the publication of the trios, Op. 1. The contract with the publishers Artaria was signed three days later, and the printed list of subscribers totalled 123 names, involving some 241 copies of the work. Prince Lichnowsky may well have subsidised the whole operation, if what Artaria's son said subsequently was correct. Certainly Lichnowsky had witnessed the first performance of the trios in his house, and he was the dedicatee.

Some time during the course of the year Beethoven's youngest brother, Nikolaus Johann, arrived in Vienna, and started to attend the university. He had been apprenticed to a pharmaceutical chemist in Bonn before leaving, and after qualifying in Vienna once more took on employment in a chemist's shop. Eventually he moved to Linz and bought his own business. Initially, however, Ludwig kept a fatherly eye on his young brother, especially as far as his morals were concerned.

As 1795 progressed, so did Ludwig's career. On St Cecilia's Day, 22 November, an annual ball took place for the pension fund of the society of artists. In the past Haydn and Mozart had both composed music for this occasion, which was held in the Redoutensaal. Usually two composers were asked to provide the music, one for the large room and one for the small. Süssmayr, who was now royal and imperial Kapellmeister, composed the music this year for the large room, and Beethoven for the small. It was a considerable tribute to his reputation, and it may have been Haydn – who had returned to Vienna from London towards the end of the summer – who was responsible for getting Beethoven the commission. The works he composed were the twelve

Salieri (1750-1825). Beethoven studied vocal writing with him and by way of acknowledgment dedicated the three sonatas for violin and piano of Op. 12 (1799) to Salieri.

minuets, WoO. 7, and twelve German dances, WoO. 8. Certainly Beethoven and Haydn worked together quite a lot at this time, for on 16 December the *Wiener Zeitung* announced that Haydn would give three of the Salomon symphonies that had been composed in London, together with a performance by Beethoven of his Op. 19 piano concerto, at a concert in the Redoutensaal. Then on 8 January 1796 Haydn and Beethoven again collaborated in a benefit concert for the singer Maria Bolla.

By 19 February, however, Beethoven was in Prague with Prince Lichnowsky, on a tour that was–from a letter he wrote to his brother Nikolaus Johann, at the time–intended to include Dresden, Leipzig, as well as Berlin, and bring in a lot of money. There is some doubt about the exact timing of the composer's movements, for it seems possible that he made a brief return to Vienna from Prague before going on with the rest of the tour. At all events it was in Prague that he composed the *scena* 'Ah, perfido!', Op. 65, for Josephine, Countess von Clary. This became a favourite in the repertoire of Josepha Duschek, the dramatic soprano who had been a friend of Mozart. Certainly she appears to have sung it at a concert in Leipzig on 21 November 1796.

We have few details of Beethoven's visit either to Dresden or Leipzig, except that he spent about eight days in the first city either in late April or early May, and received a gold snuffbox from the Elector of Saxony for his performance on the pianoforte. We have more information about him in Berlin, where he played to Friedrich Wilhelm II, King of Prussia, met the pianist Friedrich Heinrich Himmel (and subsequently fell out with him), and composed the cello sonatas, Op. 5, for Jean-Pierre Duport, a virtuoso in the royal establishment. The king gave Beethoven another gold snuffbox on his departure, this one filled with gold coins. The composer noted with pride that it was no ordinary snuffbox, but the sort normally given to ambassadors. It may well be that on this occasion the king also invited him to join his musical establishment, but Beethoven declined the invitation, and the king died in the following year, so one may never know with certainty. At all events, Carl Czerny maintained as much in a letter written some years later.

Beethoven also attended at least two meetings of the Singakademie, at which he listened to some choral works and then improvised for the assembly. He later told Madame von Arnim (at that time Elizabeth Brentano) that when he had finished playing on that occasion the listeners did not break into applause but

J. G. Albrechtsberger (1736-1809), in a lithograph portrait by H. E. von Wintter dating from 1815. After Haydn left Vienna for London again, Beethoven went to Albrechtsberger for counterpoint lessons.

The Kohlmarkt in Vienna, drawn by A. Leithner and engraved by Wett. The publishing house of Artaria is on the right.

crowded round him with tears in their eyes. He said that he told them to desist, since performers (referring to himself) did not want to hear weeping, but applause. It is possible that on the way back to Vienna he performed in Pressburg (now Bratislava in Czechoslovakia), or more probably that he went there and to Budapest shortly after his return from Berlin.

If Beethoven now seemed to be finding a place in the sun, ominous storm clouds were gathering in the south, as the victorious young French general Napoleon Bonaparte pursued his brilliant career in Italy, but all through the winter Beethoven went on working in Vienna, and in February and April 1797 Artaria announced the publication of the cello sonatas, Op. 5; the piano sonata for four hands, Op. 6; the trio for violin, viola and cello, Op. 3; the string quintet, Op. 4 (an arrangement of an earlier work, the octet for wind instruments, subsequently given the number of Op. 103), and the twelve piano variations on a Russian dance from *Das Waldmädchen*, WoO. 71. Then on 6 April Schuppanzigh gave a concert in the course of which one of Beethoven's arias was sung, and a quintet for piano and wind instruments, Op. 16, was performed.

Then suddenly, in early April, Napoleon was advancing on Vienna, and the very day after Schuppanzigh's concert the Landsturm had to be called out,

and it looked as if there would be fighting. There was a burst of patriotic fervour, though Beethoven failed signally to produce a patriotic song for the occasion that caught on. Banners were dedicated on 17 April, and all seemed ready for a confrontation, when a preliminary peace treaty was signed at Löben the next day. Three weeks later the armies were disbanded, but the crisis had passed only temporarily.

We have little precise information about Beethoven for much of the rest of 1797. There is a letter to Franz Gerhard Wegeler dated from Vienna on 29 May, in which the composer refers to recovery from an illness, and then a dedication to Lenz (Lorenz) von Breuning from Vienna dated 1 October, in an album given to him when he left Vienna in the autumn of that year, after studying medicine in the city. Beethoven continued composing and preparing work for the press, however, for on 7 October Artaria announced the piano sonata, Op. 7, and the serenade for violin, viola and cello, Op. 8, and also dating from this year was their publication of the piano rondo in C, Op. 51, No. 1.

Other compositions and publications from this year were the twelve variations for piano and cello on a theme from Handel's *Judas Maccabaeus*, WoO. 45 (dedicated to Princess Lichnowsky), and the song *Adelaide*, Op. 46, which must have been written earlier. At a concert on 23 December the variations (WoO. 28) for two oboes and horn on *Là ci darem* from Mozart's *Don Giovanni* were given at a benefit concert in Vienna, so they were certainly composed in the period leading up to Christmas, if not earlier.

The next two years – 1798 and 1799 – are even more thinly documented than the foregoing. The letters are few and far between, and in any case they are scarcely very revealing, except insofar as they confirm the very intimate nature of the terms Beethoven used in his letters to Zmeskall. On the other hand, we know that Beethoven was increasing his circle of friends among the music-loving aristocracy. In particular one must mention here the princes of Schwarzenberg and Liechtenstein, as well as Odescalchi, and the younger brother of Prince Lichnowsky, Count Moritz. It was in Prince von Schwarzenberg's palace in Vienna, for example, that Haydn's *Creation* was first heard in 1798, and where Beethoven's septet for violin, viola, clarinet, horn, bassoon, cello and double bass, Op. 20, received its first performance, after which, in direct reference to Haydn, Beethoven remarked: 'That is my creation.'

During the course of 1798 Beethoven also made a very successful visit to Prague, where he gave a performance of the piano concerto in B flat, Op. 19. It may have been on this occasion that he used the revised version of the finale that is usually heard today, rather than the rondo (WoO. 6) that constituted the original finale. He may also have given the first performance on this occasion of the piano concerto in C, Op. 15. There is an element of doubt, however, since it is later than the B flat concerto, in spite of its earlier opus number. At all events, with the completion of the *Pathétique* sonata, Op. 13, things would never be the same as far as the piano was concerned.

In the last decades of the eighteenth century the harpsichord lost ground rapidly to the piano, despite the fact that the early pianos were much softer in tone and less powerful than the ones we know today. Initially the harpsichord makers tried to compete, with the addition of such features as the Venetian swell, rather on the lines of the swell box in pipe organs. Basically the principle is that one part of the instrument is enclosed in a shuttered compartment so that the sound may be kept in, and released gradually as pressure is applied to a pedal, which in turn opens the shutters. In this way it was possible to give the harpsichord, which is a plucked stringed instrument, a degree of diminuendo and crescendo of a sort mainly possible only on an instrument with sustaining ability, such as the piano. In this context, however, it ought to be pointed out that what is usually known as the 'loud' pedal on a piano is not a device to increase the actual degree of loudness of the instrument, but to lift the damping element from the strings and allow them to vibrate freely. In this respect they appear to sound more loud.

The harpsichord was really fighting a losing battle, however, for it could in no way compete with the piano

F. G. Wegeler (1765-1848), was one of Beethoven's closest friends in Bonn, and married another close friend, Eleonore von Breuning. At the age of twenty-nine Wegeler was Rector of Bonn University, but was obliged to flee when the French occupied the Rhineland in 1794. When he reached Vienna, however, he renewed his friendship with the composer over the next two years, and eventually he worked with F. Ries to produce the Biographical Notices *of 1838.*

from a mechanical point of view, and ought really not to have tried. Such an instrument, therefore, as the harpsichord of 1782 made by Burkat Shudi and John Broadwood in London, and now in the Victoria and Albert Museum, was something of a prehistoric monster by the time it was built. However, it took time for developments to filter through and tastes to evolve, and one must bear in mind that the early pianos for which Beethoven composed were very unlike the concert grands of today. Indeed, one may well wonder whether he would have written some of the very thick textures that one sometimes finds in his piano music if he had known what the instruments would ultimately be capable of.

What was exciting, and Beethoven must have been aware of this, too, was that he was composing for the instrument more or less as it took its place in society. Although the following was written much later, we can nevertheless appreciate something of this from what Czerny, a pupil of Beethoven in his youth, subsequently wrote about his conversation with Beethoven on the matter:

> Beethoven told me, too, that he had heard Mozart play often, and that because when he was alive the fortepiano was still a very young

invention, Mozart was in the habit of playing in a way that was more appropriate to the more usual harpsichords, which was by no means appropriate to the fortepiano. Later I met many people who studied with Mozart, and I discovered that their manner of playing confirmed this.

Czerny then went on to be even more categorical, and say that the characteristics of Mozart's style were clear and decidedly brilliant playing that was much more staccato than legato. The whole approach might be described as witty and lively, and the pedal was rarely brought into play, and was never actually necessary in this style.

Beethoven, on the other hand, used the pedal a great deal, and had a very characteristic way of playing. In particular Czerny mentioned legato chords and a very cantabile, or singing, tone. By comparison with other pianists, therefore, Beethoven's technique lacked the clarity, brilliance and elegance that were their habitual manner, but nevertheless he had great spirit and breadth of interpretation, full of feeling – in a word, romantic. One might add that at times Beethoven's technique was consequently less than totally accurate, at any rate by modern standards. This was certainly the opinion of a writer in the *Allgemeine Musikalische Zeitung*

on 22 April 1799, when comparing Beethoven with the pianist Joseph Wölffl:

> Beethoven's playing is very brilliant but he is less delicate [than Wölffl] and at times he is culpable of being indistinct. He is at his best when improvising ... Since the death of Mozart, who as far as I am concerned remains the *non plus ultra*, I have never experienced this sort of pleasure to the extent that it is offered by Beethoven. Here Wölffl does not touch him. Wölffl nevertheless has advantages ... he plays seemingly impossible passages with amazing ease, precision and clarity (naturally in this he is assisted by the largeness of his hands) ...

An additional point in favour of Wölffl was that he took pains to charm his audience, whereas Beethoven's deportment was pronounced decidedly haughty.

Yet another pianist to arrive in Vienna in 1799 was John Baptist Cramer (1771-1858), and he seems to have been the only person, according to Ries, whom Beethoven regarded as distinguished in the business of piano playing. Although he was born in Mannheim, Cramer was brought up and educated in England. He went to Vienna in 1799 as part of his musical education, and to renew the acquaintance he had made with Haydn when

In 1796 Beethoven went on a tour with Prince Lichnowsky that included visits to Leipzig, left, and Dresden, above, where the Elector of Saxony made him a present of a gold snuffbox.

the latter was in England. Cramer soon met and made friends with Beethoven, and their respect for each other's playing was mutual. If Cramer was the only pianist of distinction as far as Beethoven was concerned, then Cramer maintained in later years that no one had heard extemporary piano playing unless he had heard Beethoven.

The two men were united in their admiration of Mozart. There is a story that came from Cramer's widow, to the effect that when Cramer and Beethoven were at an Augarten concert, walking together during a performance of Mozart's piano concerto in C minor (Köchel 491), Beethoven was moved to exclaim: 'Cramer, Cramer, we shall never be able to do anything like that.' Certainly Cramer admired Mozart enormously, along with Handel, and Bach's keyboard compositions, but there was a point in Beethoven's music beyond which he could not go, and this must have become increasingly difficult for Cramer as Beethoven developed his musical personality to the full. It is perhaps hard for us to put ourselves back into the mind of a

person who heard Beethoven's music for the first time. What we have come to accept as the quintessence of Beethoven, his contemporaries tended to regard as flaws, distortions – aberrations even – in his otherwise beautiful and harmonious compositions. This was less true for the young, however, for whom Beethoven spoke an exciting language – probably to the irritation of their mentors. When Cipriani Potter was praising a particular aspect of Beethoven's music to Cramer, the older man grumbled: 'If Beethoven emptied his inkstand upon a piece of music paper you would admire it.'

This is perhaps a warning to us all that we must be careful in our approach to contemporary music. One simply cannot dismiss what is being produced at any given moment in musical history as irrelevant or wrong, for to do so would be to deny any possibility of music's further growth and development beyond that moment. The result would be tantamount to putting music in a museum, and if this had happened in previous generations, imagine what masterpieces would have been lost to us today.

On the other hand, it is only fair to say that things were very different in the eighteenth century, and indeed until well into the nineteenth. Today there is a great divide between classical and contemporary music, but then the music that people listened to was almost all

Ignaz Schuppanzigh (1776-1830) was an excellent solo violinist whose physical presence matched his outsize talent, and provided the butt for a great deal of the humour that Beethoven loved to indulge in. His lasting memorial, in addition to being a close friend of Beethoven, must surely be his membership of the Razumovsky Quartet.

'contemporary'. What was 'classical' to them was either of the fairly recent past, or forgotten. Their appetite for contemporary music seemed to be insatiable, and at times it hardly seemed as if composers could keep up with their demands. An enormous amount of music making went on in the major cities of Europe such as Rome, Venice, London, Paris and Vienna, and not only for public consumption–whether it be formal occasions, theatres or concerts–but in homes of almost every degree of the social scale. In the Vienna of Beethoven's youth there were a great many wealthy aristocrats who seemed almost to live for music, and spent a fortune on it. All that was going to change eventually, as music ceased to be an adjunct to polite society, a matter for princely patronage. In the upheavals that were to shatter the old Europe and give nationalism a huge impetus, music was to play a completely different role. To explore any further at this point is to anticipate the story, but suffice it to say here that with Beethoven's music a new spirit was abroad. Romanticism was born; indeed many would credit its creation to Beethoven himself, though closer examination of the music of

Mozart and even Haydn gives some fairly clear indications of what was to come, certainly from a specifically musical point of view.

Reactions at the time varied. The Emperor Franz, as reported by Johann Dolezalek, simply said that he did not want to hear Beethoven's music or anything about it: 'There is something revolutionary in that music.' For the view of a working musician, however, we have the account of the virtuoso pianist Ignaz Moscheles (1794-1870):

> At this time [1804] I was told by some fellow pupils of mine that a young composer had come to Vienna and that he wrote very strange things impossible to play or comprehend; baroque music that went against all rules. The composer's name was Beethoven. When I returned to the library so as to satisfy my curiosity about the odd genius of that name, I came across Beethoven's *Sonate Pathétique* . . . Because my pocket money was insufficient to buy it, I copied it in secret.

Even allowing for a certain amount of reading back by a mature man to the time when he was only ten years of age, Moscheles was evidently well aware, as were many others at this time, that the *Pathétique* was something relevant, important even, and indeed the very opening C minor chord can bring Beethoven almost physically into our midst today, so characteristic is it of him, even allowing for the probable difference between the sound produced by the pianos of his day and our own.

The *Pathétique* did not come totally out of the blue, however. One must look at it in relation to what came before and after in the piano music. On 5 July 1798 Eder in Vienna published the three sonatas of Op. 10 which, if they were influenced by Clementi's piano music, are yet an important milestone in the development of Beethoven's musical personality, for even if judged only in comparison with Clementi, it is highly illuminating to see how Beethoven chose different solutions, and what those solutions were. Needless to say, the sonatas must be taken on their own merits in the last analysis, and not merely insofar as they improve on, or fall short of, the standard achieved by Clementi. In Thayer's estimation they were the first of 'the glorious series of sonatas'.

Eder also published the *Pathétique*, in 1799, and then Hoffmeister in Leipzig published it on 18 December that same year. Three days later Mollo published the two sonatas of Op. 14, so this was certainly a very intensive period of piano music composition, even if one allows that preliminary sketches for these works may have stretched back over a period of several months, if not in fact as long as one or two years. However, by now work must have been in hand for the first symphony, the first performance of which took place on 2 April 1800.

In view of this, and the time it must have taken to compose, copy out parts and then rehearse the orchestra, one is probably correct in assuming that it was begun during the course of 1799.

Before moving on to that momentous first performance of the first symphony, one ought to consider Beethoven's musical and social contacts as he was poised ready to make his next great step forward in his career. First, however, there was a great cause for regret in the late summer or early autumn of 1799, for one of Beethoven's happiest friendships had to come to an end. Karl Amenda (1771-1836) had come to Vienna in the spring of 1798. Eventually he became a pastor, for he had studied theology at Jena University, but on arrival in Vienna he first took a post as tutor to Prince Lobkowitz's children, and taught music in the home of Mozart's widow. It was whilst Amenda was playing first violin in a quartet that he became aware that someone had stationed himself by him to turn the pages for him. At the conclusion of the work, Beethoven—for that is who it was—merely made a bow and withdrew, but the next evening, when Amenda attended a reception at which Beethoven was also a guest, the host greeted him with the news that he had captured Beethoven's heart.

Of course such friendships were fashionable at the time, or at least much more common than they are in our own highly self-conscious society. Be that as it may, even allowing for the more extrovert character of relationships in those days, it is clear that Beethoven was captivated by Amenda to the degree that they were so much in each other's company that if one were seen in the streets without the other, people would ask: 'Where is the other one?'

In order to relieve the fairly regular financial crises that occurred in Beethoven's life at this time, Amenda suggested that he make a trip to Italy. Beethoven agreed to the project on condition that Amenda went with him, and the whole trip was virtually arranged when Amenda had to return home. His brother had been killed in an accident, and he had to take up his new responsibilities as the head of his family. On a copy of the string quartet in F, Op. 18, No. 1 which Beethoven gave Amenda on 25 June 1799, the composer wrote: 'Take this quartet as a small souvenir of our friendship, and whenever you play it, remember the days we spent together and the sincere affection felt for you then, and which will always be felt by Your true and warm friend . . .'

The departure of Beethoven's friend may, however, have turned out to be a blessing in disguise, for they never had occasion to quarrel, a fact on which Beethoven himself was moved to comment later. Unlike so many other friends, Amenda failed to provoke a rupture with Beethoven, whether wittingly or unwittingly,

Count Moritz Lichnowsky, brother of Beethoven's patron Prince Karl, was almost as devoted to the composer and his music as his brother, and did much to help him. He died in 1837.

J. B. Cramer (1771-1858), in a lithograph portrait, c. 1815. Cramer was a distinguished pianist who went to Vienna in 1799, and was one of the few exponents whose talent Beethoven readily acknowledged. The two men also had in common their great admiration of Mozart.

and in defence of Beethoven's friends one must say that very often it was unwittingly.

In a letter written to Amenda, presumably during the course of the summer before he left for his home in Courland (later East Prussia, and now part of the USSR), Beethoven confided to his friend that his heart had been deeply wounded, and that he was going to the village of Mödling for a few days. The worst was over, he wrote, and he felt that this spell away from Vienna would help him to get over the disappointment he had suffered, and see his way more clearly for the immediate future. It has been suggested that Beethoven proposed to Magdalena Willmann, a singer then in Vienna, but she had not responded favourably to his proposal. There was certainly a tradition in the Willmann family that she would not even consider Beethoven because he was so ugly and half mad. Doubtless other people held the same opinion, but the Willmanns had come from Bonn, so their judgment may well have been coloured by having known the Beethoven family in general, and Ludwig in particular, of old.

Then there were other women with whom Beethoven was in fairly regular contact, such as the soprano Christine Gerhardi, and the wives and daughters of the nobility who patronised or befriended him. With these, however, his relationships were by no means so intense, except for the person who was the recipient of the letters addressed to the Immortal Beloved, and whose identity we will consider in due course. Suffice it to mention here one or two noble ladies who were recipients of dedications, such as Anna Louisa Barbara (Babette), daughter of Karl, Count Keglevics de Busin, to whom Beethoven dedicated the piano sonata, Op. 7; the piano variations on *La stessa, la stessissima*, WoO 73, and the piano concerto in C, Op. 15. By the time Beethoven came to dedicate the last-named work, Babette had become Princess Odescalchi, and the composer was a participant in the musical soirées at the Odescalchi Palace. There was also Henriette, the sister of Prince Karl Lichnowsky, to whom Beethoven dedicated the piano rondo in G, Op. 51, No. 2 – in the second place, that is, for he had first dedicated it to Countess Giulietta Guicciardi, but then exchanged it for the C sharp minor piano sonata, Op. 27, No. 2, the *Moonlight*, as we shall see presently.

Before leaving this topic, one might also mention the dedication of the clarinet trio, Op. 11, to the mother of Prince Karl Lichnowsky, Countess Thun, and the piano sonata in E flat, Op. 27, No. 1 to Josepha Sophia, wife of Prince Johann von Liechtenstein. Finally, there was Baroness Braun, to whom Beethoven dedicated the two piano sonatas, Op. 14, and the sonata for horn, Op. 17, whose husband leased the Nationaltheater and afterwards the Theater an der Wien, which was to have significance later when Beethoven was asked to write

an opera. This Baroness Braun must not be confused with Countess Browne, to whom Beethoven dedicated the three piano sonatas, Op. 10, and the *Waldmädchen* piano variations, WoO. 71. This lady's husband, Count Browne, whom Beethoven described as his first Maecenas, was in fact a Russian, despite his name.

As an immediate prelude to the composition of the first symphony – purely technical elements of extended composition apart – one must consider how Beethoven acquired his experience of scoring and his knowledge of instrumentation in general. Naturally there was his family background to start with, and his own experience, both as a child violinist and then working with orchestras in Bonn. On his arrival in Vienna much of his music making at first was with a chamber group, and in particular Beethoven had the benefit of the experience of Schuppanzigh and his friends, whom we have already encountered. Then during the course of 1799 Beethoven met the virtuoso double bass player Domenico Dragonetti, who so pleased Beethoven with his playing of the sonata for cello and piano, Op. 5, No. 2, that

K. F. Amenda (1771-1836) studied theology at Jena University, and eventually became a pastor, but was in Vienna during 1798 and 1799 as a tutor, and so struck up a deep and lasting friendship with Beethoven – one of the very few that were not marred by the composer's difficult nature.

The pianist Daniel Steibelt (1765-1823), who was born in Berlin, and was one of the first to make himself an international career as a concert performer. In 1800 he went to Vienna, where he and Beethoven competed in a somewhat unedifying trial of virtuosity at the house of Count Fries.

when they reached the end of the piece, the composer jumped up from the keyboard and threw his arms round both player and instrument.

As far as the horn was concerned, it was Johann Wenzel Stich, who italianised his name to Giovanni Punto, who showed Beethoven the instrument's possibilities, though the players Hradezky and Herbst are also mentioned as having helped. As far as the flute was concerned it was Karl Scholl, especially in the early 1800s, when the instrument was still evolving. Other names traditionally mentioned are Friedlowsky for the clarinet, and Czerwensky for the oboe. Not, of course, that Beethoven always took their advice. When Kraft complained to him that it was not possible to play a certain passage on the cello, the composer merely retorted: 'It has to be,' and when other instrumentalists complained that they had been given things that were too difficult to play, if not impossible, Beethoven merely pointed to those who could play, or had played, the passage, and remarked that if the others could do it, then they must, too.

Schubert faced much the same problem with his Great symphony, certainly as far as the wind instrumentalists were concerned. One must remember, however, that it was a time when many technical developments were taking place in the mechanism and construction of instruments, and it was only by the mutual interaction of players, manufacturers and composers that these developments were explored and exploited to the full. Had Beethoven and Schubert not made the demands they did, the progress and resulting benefits would have evolved over a much longer period.

It was a matter that concerned Beethoven, particularly with respect to the piano, which was after all the instrument he first became known by, and in a letter to the piano maker Johann Andreas Streicher, written about three years previously, Beethoven had remarked:

No doubt the manner of playing the piano is so far the least developed kind of instrumental playing. Frequently one thinks that one is hearing a harp, and I am glad, my dear friend,

that you are one of the few who understand and feel that it is also possible to sing on the piano, provided one has feeling. I hope the time will come when harp and piano will be considered two quite different instruments.

In that wish, at least, Beethoven was to be gratified. A much larger wish was soon to be gratified, however, and that was his concert in Vienna on 2 April 1800, in the Burgtheater.

There were seven items advertised for the programme, namely a Mozart symphony, an aria from Haydn's *Creation*, a piano concerto composed and played by Beethoven, a septet composed by Beethoven and dedicated to the Empress Maria-Theresa (the wife of Emperor Franz), a duet from Haydn's *Creation*, improvisation on the piano by Beethoven, and finally a symphony by Beethoven. This seemingly marathon programme was to begin at 6.30 p.m. There is an element of doubt as to whether the piano concerto was the one in C, Op. 15, but there is no doubt that the symphony was No. 1 in C, Op. 21. In its report of the concert the *Allgemeine Musikalische Zeitung* said that it was the most interesting one of its kind held for a long time, and praised in particular the first two movements of the concerto, the 'taste and feeling' in the septet, the

mastery of the improvisation, and the composition of the symphony which exhibited 'much art, novelty and wealth of ideas'. The only criticism of the music itself was that there was too much use of the wind instruments in the symphony, so that it sounded like a wind band rather than an orchestra. In including works by Mozart and Haydn, Beethoven was paying tribute to his two great predecessors, which can only have helped him in the eyes of the Viennese concert-going public, but in fact he was also associating his talent with theirs, and laying claim to his position as their successor.

Beethoven's success was unquestioned, but the orchestra came in for some pretty harsh words from the reviewer. There had been quarrels beforehand over who was to conduct, and this had not helped to conceal the shortcomings of the orchestra, especially since it was obvious that Beethoven's music was not easy to play. They paid little attention to the soloist in the concerto, and in the second movement of the symphony did not even bother to watch the beat. Of what use, then, as the reviewer rightly asked in a somewhat rhetorical vein, was their skill?

Just over two weeks after this concert Beethoven again appeared in public, this time with the horn virtuoso Stich, alias Punto. The composer agreed to write a sonata for horn and piano, Op. 17, for the occasion, and it was so well received that it was repeated again immediately as an encore. Then towards the end of the month, 27 April to be precise, and the sixteenth anniversary of his entry into Bonn, Maximilian Franz arrived in Vienna with a small suite. He hardly had another year to live, though it was not obvious at the time, and in this last period of his somewhat doomed existence, his greatest wish was to visit America. This may seem a little strange, but one must not underestimate the fascination, amounting almost to inspiration, that America presented to enlightened minds at the end of the eighteenth century and the early years of the nineteenth.

Also in the course of this month, or possibly in May, the pianist Daniel Steibelt came to Vienna flushed with the triumph of a concert in Prague that was said to have made him 1,800 florins. It was more or less inevitable that the two pianists—Beethoven and Steibelt—should have encountered each other, but the way in which they did was particularly unfortunate, for it merely goaded them on to compete with each other in a rather humiliating way at Count Fries's house. At their second 'duel', again at Count Fries's, Beethoven is reputed to have been so incensed by Steibelt's behaviour that he took the cello part of the latter's quintet that had been performed that evening, placed it upside down on the piano stand, drummed out a theme from the first few bars with one finger, then proceeded to improvise. Steibelt would not wait until the end, and refused to meet Beethoven again. He even went so far as to ensure, whenever he accepted an invitation, that Beethoven would not be there.

After this somewhat hectic spring, Beethoven moved out of Vienna for the summer of 1800 to Unterdöbling, about an hour's walk from the city, and took accommodation in the same house as the wife and children of a Viennese lawyer. The name of the family was Grillparzer, and one of the children was destined to grow up to be a poet, and eventually write Beethoven's funeral oration. At this time Beethoven still practised hard to perfect his piano technique, and Madame Grillparzer loved to listen outside his door, until one day he must have had a premonition that someone was there, for he jumped up, flung open the door, and discovered

Opposite: the interior of the Burgtheater in Vienna, where Beethoven gave his first public benefit concert in the city on 2 April 1800. One of the works on the programme was the septet, Op. 20. A facsimile is reproduced below.

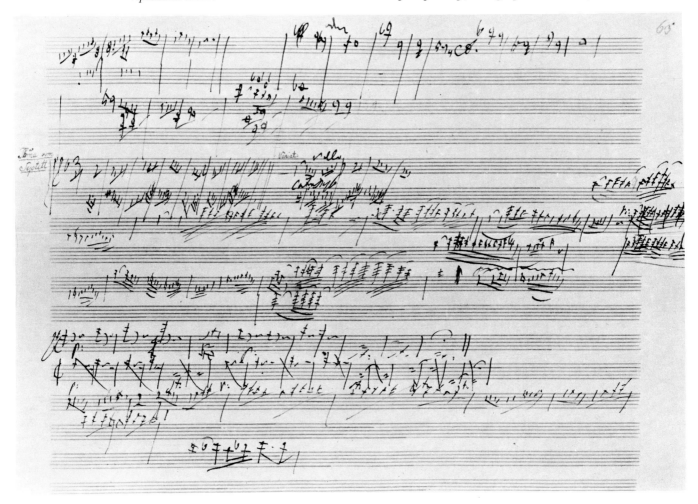

the unfortunate woman. After that he played no more, or so the story goes. There is also the possibility that the whole incident ought to be placed rather in 1808, since in his own writings Grillparzer maintained that he first met Beethoven during a musical evening at the home of his uncle, Joseph Sonnleithner, in 1804 or 1805.

One happy product of this summer was probably the C minor piano concerto, Op. 37, for the composer himself put the year 1800 on it, though it was not published until November 1804. Then there were also the six string quartets of Op. 18 which, even if they had been begun a year or so previously, were completed during the course of 1800. Unfortunately Beethoven's own correspondence for this year is pitifully scarce. We have only two notes to Zmeskall–which may belong to this year, but are by no means to be included here with any certainty, for they have no dates–and two other letters which are dated. The first is to Friedrich von Matthisson, whose poem *Adelaide* Beethoven had set

with such success. In the letter he told Matthisson of his dedication of the work to him, and apologised for not having written to him sooner. The work had in fact been published in February 1797. Beethoven maintained that the reason was twofold. He did not know where Matthisson was living at the time, and he was too shy to write at first, since he did not know whether the work would have met with the poet's approval. He asked Matthisson to send him his next poem 'immediately' for setting, though after more than three years one might well ask why such haste. In the event Beethoven did set at least three more of Matthisson's works, though not with quite the same success as the first.

The other letter from this year dates from 15 December, and is much more interesting from a documentary point of view. It is to Franz Anton Hoffmeister, who left Vienna in 1800 to go to Leipzig and set up the music publishing house that eventually became C. F. Peters in 1814. In the letter Beethoven expressed regret that he had not known sooner of Hoffmeister's intention, for he would have entrusted to him the publication of the Op. 18 quartets which were to come out in two instalments in June and October next year (1801) from

The title page of Beethoven's Op. 19, the piano concerto in B flat, which was dedicated to C. Nikl and published in Vienna by Hoffmeister.

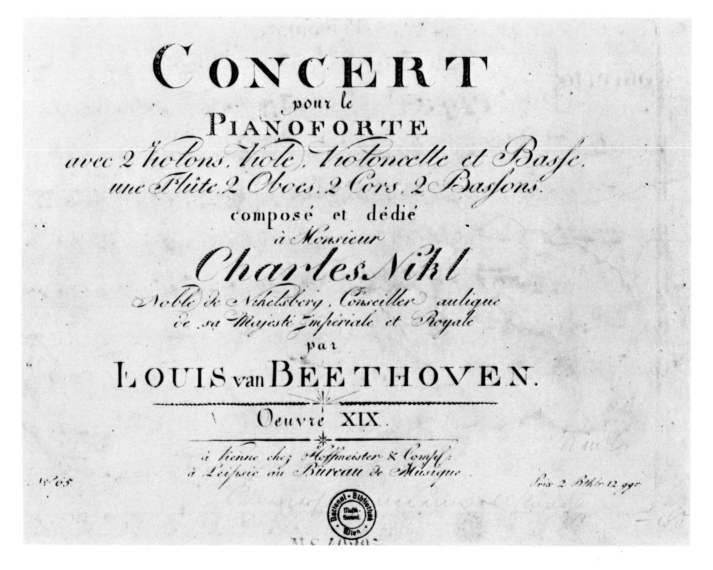

Mollo in Vienna. However, Beethoven was prepared to let him have the septet, Op. 20; the first symphony, Op. 21; the B flat piano concerto, Op. 19; the B flat piano sonata, Op. 22, and promised for later the string quintet in C, Op. 29, though in the end it was not Hoffmeister who published it after all, but Breitkopf & Härtel. The composer was quite candid in remarking that he did not consider the piano concerto one of his best – Mollo was to publish the Op. 15 piano concerto in C in March the following year – but he had better works in reserve until he made the journey, presumably to Leipzig, himself. In referring to the septet Beethoven remarked that all the instruments were obbligati, and went on to comment that he was incapable of composing anything that was not obbligato, seeing that he had come into the world with an obbligato accompaniment. This is now taken to be a reference to the fact that he was born with a caul.

We find Beethoven writing to Hoffmeister again on 15 January 1801 'or thereabouts' as the composer himself put on his letter, about the same works, but this time the two men have begun to discuss terms. Beethoven found it all rather tiresome, largely because he did not like having to handle figures – something which he was far from good at in any case – but also because he found the whole concept of artists having to market their wares tiresome. There is no reason to doubt his sincerity in this matter. He would have been perfectly content, as he said in his letter, for there to have been a market somewhere in the world to which the artist brought his work and in return received sufficient remuneration to satisfy his needs. Beethoven was also delighted to learn that Hoffmeister was going to publish some of the keyboard works of J. S. Bach. That, he felt, was really an undertaking of merit and worth.

Later that month Beethoven agreed to participate in a charity concert organised by Christine Gerhardi-Frank to benefit the wounded of the Battle of Hohenlinden, which had taken place on 3 December 1800. Baron von Braun had organised a performance of Haydn's *Creation* on 16 January, conducted by the composer himself, and Madame Frank's concert was due to take place on 30 January. The other artistes involved were to be the organiser, Madame Galvani (Magdalena Willmann) and Herr Simoni as vocalists, Beethoven and Punto as the instrumentalists, with Haydn conducting two of his symphonies, and Paër and Conti conducting the orchestras for the vocal items.

With such a distinguished cast assembled it came therefore as something of a shock to the participants, who were lending their professional standing to help a worthy cause, when they discovered that in the first public announcement of the concert only one artiste's name was mentioned, and that was the name of the organiser, 'the famous amateur singer Frau von Frank,

E. G. Haussmann's portrait of J. S. Bach (1685-1750), whose works Hoffmeister published in an edition to which Beethoven subscribed, and persuaded his patron Prince Lichnowsky to do likewise. Beethoven much admired Bach's music, and always intended doing something to help the plight of his then surviving daughter, who was living in poverty.

née Gerhardi'. Beethoven's letter to her is a masterpiece of controlled rage and fury. For once his rather disjointed epistolary style is highly effective, and its spontaneous quality breathes, even at this distance, what must have been Beethoven's anger – and that of his colleagues – when they discovered what had happened. In his letter Beethoven suggested that it might have been her husband's responsibility, or that the omission had been due to haste or forgetfulness, but it is hard to believe that he really thought that. The atmosphere can hardly have been a good one in which to mount a concert, and we do not know what the performance was like eventually. Certainly the facts would seem to suggest that the auspices were not good, for when the advertisement appeared on 24 and 28 January, it still had not been altered. It was not the first time that an unscrupulous and ambitious person had climbed to success over the backs of fellow artists, and it was by no means going to be the last.

However, Beethoven had other things to occupy his mind from this time. He had been approached by Salvatore Viganò to write a ballet for the court company, the subject of which was to be 'The Creatures of

Prometheus'. It received its first performance on 28 March, though from a letter to Hoffmeister of 22 April, Beethoven was not entirely happy with the way in which Viganò mounted the ballet, and as an example of Beethoven's composition, the ballet music has been rather neglected in the past. But the scoring has effects that surely rank among some of his most enchanting.

We also learn from this letter to Hoffmeister that Beethoven had decided to become a subscriber to the J. S. Bach works, and had persuaded Prince Lichnowsky to do likewise. On the same day Beethoven also wrote to another publisher, this time Breitkopf & Härtel in Leipzig. The firm had approached him with a view to publishing some of his music, but at that time Beethoven had nothing that he felt was particularly suitable, since both Mollo and Hoffmeister had just published or were about to publish his music, and in any case Beethoven was not clear as to what sort of works Breitkopf & Härtel were particularly interested in. There was also the question of the musical review, *Allgemeine Musikalische Zeitung*, which was published by the same firm. Beethoven seems to have been attempting to counter adverse criticism of his music, as published in the review. Mollo had published the Op. 15 piano concerto the previous month, and Hoffmeister was to publish the Op. 19 piano concerto in the December of 1801. Beethoven said that he was quite aware that neither of these was his best composition, nor was he above receiving adverse criticism. Even so, he had obviously been mortified, and only managed to take comfort from that fact that when he compared what they said about other Viennese composers, he came to the conclusion that the reviewers in Leipzig knew nothing about music. An easy sort of comfort to take one might think, but at the same time Beethoven made a point which is as valid today as it was then, namely that if an established composer such as Beethoven had now become was affected by such criticism, what hope was there for a beginner? In Beethoven's case he could afford to be philosophical about it, but a younger composer might simply be frightened off for ever.

Nevertheless Beethoven closed the letter on a better note. He wanted peace, he said, between them, and he went on to refer to the appeal that had been launched in the *Allgemeine Musikalische Zeitung* for Bach's only surviving child, Regine Susanna, who was living in poverty. Beethoven said that he was amazed and disappointed at the small amount that had come from Germany – not only the German-speaking countries as a whole but the Germany proper in which Leipzig was situated. Beethoven then proposed to Breitkopf & Härtel that he himself should publish something by subscription, for the daughter's benefit, though even here he was all too aware of human nature, and felt that

in order to protect himself against possible charges in the future that he was misappropriating funds, he proposed issuing an annual report of the profit made. In the event the project does not seem to have come to anything.

At this point the Elector Maximilian Franz came back into Beethoven's life for the last time. He had finally settled at Hetzendorf, just outside Vienna, and by the beginning of June his health was giving cause for concern. So much so, in fact, that a chapter of the Teutonic Order, of which Maximilian Franz was Grand Master, was called for 1 June. This had the beneficial effect, as far as Beethoven was concerned, of bringing Stephan von Breuning to Vienna, since he was an official of the order, and it may well be that another old Bonn friend, Anton Reicha, also came to Vienna at this time. It may also be because of Maximilian Franz's health that Beethoven chose Hetzendorf as his summer retreat that year, since it was by no means one of the more attractive places around Vienna that he might have decided upon.

From a letter that Beethoven must have written to Hoffmeister about 21 June 1801, since it arrived in Leipzig on 29 June that year, Beethoven still intended dedicating his first symphony to the elector. Just over a month later, on 26 July, Maximilian Franz was dead, and later the composer dedicated the work to Baron von Swieten. Other works probably completed by this time were the sonatas for piano and violin, Op. 23 and Op. 24 (published on 28 October); the piano sonata in A flat, Op. 26; the piano sonatas in E flat and C sharp minor, Op. 27, No. 1 and No. 2 respectively; the piano sonata in D, Op. 28, and the string quintet in C, Op. 29. Czerny maintained that the slow movement of the Op. 28 sonata was Beethoven's favourite, and that he often played it for his own pleasure. The C sharp minor sonata, Op. 27, No. 2, is of course the well-known *Moonlight* sonata. Obviously the work has enormous appeal, especially the first movement, and in particular to people who do not come easily to what they would probably regard as 'classical' music. Even so, its popularity – even in the composer's own lifetime – has tended to eclipse other works worthy of being better known. Beethoven himself felt that the F sharp piano sonata, Op. 78, for example, was a much better work.

For some composers there have always been individual works which have become enormously popular – one thinks in the present century of Ravel's *Bolero* by comparison with his *Chansons Madécasses*, which were more important to him from the point of view of what he was trying to say, but which were unfortunately ahead of their time. It is one of the facts of the creative *métier* that artists have to learn to live with. Where it is particularly regrettable, however, is when a composer becomes known only for one work or sort of work, and this may act as a deterrent to those who identify him only with that work, and never explore further. There are of course several of Beethoven's compositions that one would not place high on a list of works through which a newcomer might be introduced to his music if one did not wish to deter him. But equally one ought not to try and pretend that these works did not happen, or do not exist, since they are an essential part of the process that resulted in the masterpieces.

One of the effects of the Romantic movement in music in particular, though to some extent the same holds good for all art forms, was that inspiration somehow tended to come to be regarded as more important in the creative process than the act of writing the music down. In other words, only masterpieces counted, and everything else might be dismissed out of hand. Certainly some fundamental misconceptions that are still with us spread in the post-Beethoven period – that genius and inspiration somehow obliterated the need for craftsmanship and sheer hard work, or indeed that if hard work was required, then the composer in question was not truly 'great'. If one looks closely at the way that Beethoven worked at his compositions, that view ought to be dispelled at once. Even at the time of which we are writing, the summer of 1801, he was capable of writing in all honesty that he had only just learnt how

to write quartets, and that his piano playing had improved considerably – when he was openly acknowledged as one of the foremost composers and virtuoso pianists of the day. We see from this, however, that he was conscious of the need to improve, and that he was unlikely to rest on his laurels and feel no further need to work.

Seen in this context, his exception to the treatment he had received at the hands of the critics was much more the feeling that he had been misjudged and misunderstood by people whose opinion was propagated to all and sundry, and was of doubtful worth in any case, rather than that his reputation or professional standing had been viciously or jealously undermined in some way. Inevitably, however, one must relate this to the much wider context of his own life, and in this Beethoven must obviously have been experiencing the most serious and potentially undermining crisis of his life so far. By the month of June 1801 it was quite obvious to Beethoven – though he hoped that no one else had yet become aware of it – that he was having trouble with his hearing. Fate seemed to have dealt him the most cruel blow, that at the very moment of his taking his place as the successor to Mozart and Haydn, he should be robbed of so important a part of his apparatus as a musician.

The title page of Cappi's edition of the Moonlight Sonata, Op. 27, No. 2, showing the dedication to Giulietta Guicciardi.

43

Heiligenstadt

THE FIRST intimation we have of Beethoven's deafness is contained in two letters that date from late June and early July 1801. One is to Franz Gerhard Wegeler in Bonn, and the other to Karl Amenda in Courland. The very choice of these two men is in itself significant, for they were probably the only two in whom the composer felt able to confide what was obviously a terrible secret for a man in his situation to have to keep to himself.

From both letters we learn that in the previous year Prince Lichnowsky had arranged for a sum of 600 florins to be paid annually to Beethoven, and that the composer was now making money from his compositions. In fact he was now offered more commissions than he could cope with, and when he had something ready for publication there were always six or seven publishers eager to obtain the work. He no longer had to haggle over prices, he said. Now he simply stated his price and they paid. However, it seemed as if Fate was jealous of him, and instead of being able to enjoy this state of freedom from financial worry, he had been struck down.

In the letter to Wegeler he stated that he had been conscious that his hearing had been getting weaker over the previous three years–in other words from the middle of 1798–and in the letter to Amenda he stated that it had begun to be evident whilst Amenda was still in Vienna–that is up until the summer of 1799–but he had said nothing. The doctors had connected his deafness with his stomach condition, which apparently dated back to his time in Bonn, as Beethoven reminded Wegeler, but today the evidence points to the fact that the two were quite independent. An attack of typhus could also have damaged the nerves required for hearing, though at present the majority of experts suggest that his deafness was caused by otosclerosis, the growth of a spongy bone inside the ear. Nowadays it is possible to operate for this condition, or even a hearing aid may be sufficient; at that time, however, there was little of any practical value that could be done.

As to the recurrent stomach trouble, there were moments when it was especially bad, though in the period before the letter to Wegeler, who was himself a medical man, tepid Danube baths had given Beethoven some relief. It was a problem that was to remain with him, however, to the end of his life, and get progressively worse. In addition, some scholars are today of the opinion that Beethoven had syphilis, either congenital or contracted.

Naturally the physical effect of the composer's illness, but more especially the disability of his deafness, had tended to make him less keen to move about in society. Indeed in the letter to Wegeler he stated that he had been attending social functions less and less over a period of about two years. Practically, it meant that in the theatre he had to get as close as possible to the orchestra pit so as to be able to hear what the actors on stage were singing or saying, and if he was too far away he was unable to hear high notes from instruments or voices. If people spoke too softly he could hardly hear what they were saying; if they shouted, on the other hand, it was agonising for him.

To a certain degree Beethoven felt that he could avoid detection simply by accentuating his absent-mindedness; but he feared what his enemies might do to denigrate him if it became known widely in Vienna that he was deaf. For this reason he told both Wegeler and Amenda that they were to tell no one, in Wegeler's case not even Eleonore von Breuning. It was a great consolation to Beethoven, however, that Eleonore's brother Stephan was now in Vienna, and he even talked of trying to arrange for Stephan to come and live in the same house, though this did not come about yet.

The letter to Amenda shows us a more complex side of Beethoven's character, for in it he revealed a neurotic dependence on him, and an assumption of his unswerving loyalty that bordered on the possessive. Beethoven was still talking in terms of going on a tour together and imagined that Amenda would give up everything, and go and devote himself to the composer's welfare. Evidently Amenda had given Beethoven cause, through his protestations or demonstrations of loyalty and affection, to count on him. At the same time Beethoven made highly disparaging remarks about Zmeskall and Schuppanzigh, and his Viennese friends in general, for their egoism. In what is probably a reference to *Hamlet*— Beethoven had been reading Shakespeare in Schlegel's translation — he described them as instruments on which he played when he felt so inclined. In fact he valued them, so he maintained, only insofar as they were of use to him. In this respect even Prince Lichnowsky was not entirely free from denigration, despite his generosity towards the composer.

Perhaps we can make allowances for Beethoven at this point, in view of what he had to contend with, for despite professions of resignation in both letters, there is smouldering resentment as well, and in the Amenda letter a confession that he had even, on occasion, cursed God. At this point he still lived in hopes of a complete cure, since his stomach trouble was so much better, but if after six months the deafness was found to be incurable, then Beethoven hoped that Amenda would come and be his companion. A further letter to Wegeler, dated 16 November 1801, implies that Wegeler had suggested to Beethoven that he return to Bonn and live with him, but Beethoven declined. For one thing, he wrote, he would not like to see Wegeler's anxiety and pity. His hearing was no better; if anything it was worse. His stomach certainly was better, however, and generally speaking the tone of the letter is more confident and more determined. It contains the composer's famous resolution to grasp Fate by the throat, and to refuse to be crushed by it.

One of the reasons for this brighter outlook was given by Beethoven himself as one of the best of all tonics— love:

> I am now leading a rather more pleasant life, for I am living more amongst human beings. You would hardly believe how empty and sad a life I have led for the last two years. My bad hearing haunted me everywhere like a ghost and I avoided people. I seemed a misanthrope, though I am far from being one.

Heiligenstadt in the early years of the nineteenth century.

This change has been made by a dear, enchanting girl who loves me and whom I love . . . for the first time I feel that marriage might bring me happiness.

Unfortunately, as Beethoven went on to explain, he and his beloved were not of the same social class. In any case, presumably because of his deafness, he was unable to contemplate matrimony now.

Naturally there has been a great deal of speculation as to who this 'dear, enchanting girl' was, and the evidence would certainly seem to point to Countess Giulietta Guicciardi. Although she was barely seventeen at the time, she had caused a sensation when she arrived in Vienna during the course of 1800, and continued to do so. Certainly by the time Countess Josephine von Deym wrote to her sisters in January 1801, Giulietta Guicciardi was known to Viennese society as 'the beautiful Guicciardi'. She became Beethoven's piano pupil, he fell in love with her and he subsequently dedicated the *Moonlight* sonata to her.

The house in Heiligenstadt, now in the nineteenth district of Vienna, where Beethoven wrote the famous Testament in 1802 which marked his acceptance of his deafness and its implications for the rest of his life.

It was only much later, in 1823, that the interview he had with Schindler, recorded in one of the conversation books, revealed how Beethoven arranged financial aid – or so he claimed – for the man she eventually married, Count Gallenberg.

Something else which emerges from the letter to Wegeler is that Beethoven was thinking of changing from Gerhard von Vering as his physician to Johann Schmidt, and that he presumably acted on this during the course of the ensuing winter, for some time in the following April he left Vienna for the village of Heiligenstadt, on the advice of his doctor. Letters dating from April and July in 1802 to publishers Hoffmeister and Breitkopf & Härtel are addressed from Vienna, though this is probably only in a general way, since one on 13 July is headed Vienna, and one on 14 July is headed Heiligenstadt.

These letters show Beethoven in quite a businesslike mood. At times he is amusing, usually efficient, sometimes apparently listless, but at others looking forward with a strong element of hope to the future. He obviously regarded this as a period of building up his forces for the future, and in so doing was evidently taking Dr Schmidt's advice. In the event the value of that advice was questionable, since Beethoven's hearing did not

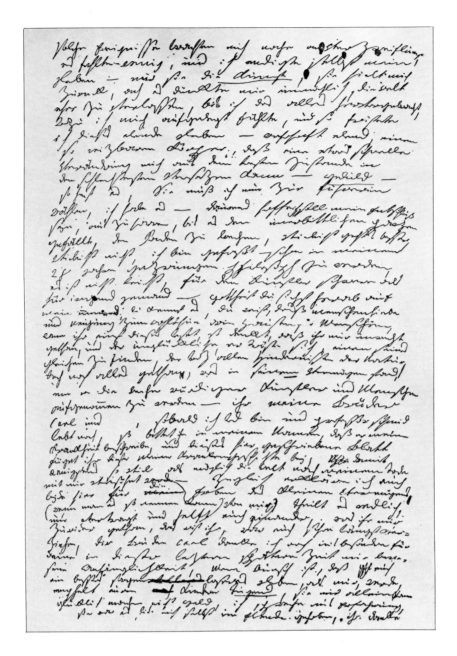

improve, and he merely withdrew from society, still no doubt convinced that the secret of his deafness was safe, at a time when he would have been more profitably employed, if one may put it that way, in coming to terms with his disability and in trying to begin relating to the society he was so earnestly shunning. Consequently, in his loneliness at Heiligenstadt, he had a great deal of time for reflection which took him through the Valley of the Shadow of Death, and to the brink of suicide.

All of this is contained in the remarkable document, found after his death, known as the Heiligenstadt Testament, which Beethoven himself dated 6 October 1802, with an addition dated 10 October. There is a strong temptation, which unfortunately must be resisted, to reproduce the document in full. It is addressed to Beethoven's brothers, though there is a blank where Johann's name should be, and begins as a plea for understanding in view of his great disability, which he now says may be permanent, and which has been with him for six years, which would put it back to some time in 1796. He is not the misanthrope he seems—on the contrary, he has always been full of goodwill towards mankind in general, but he is simply incapable of saying to people: 'Speak louder, shout, for I am deaf!' He then draws a picture, corroborated by Ferdinand Ries, of being with a friend in the country, and being unable to hear a shepherd's flute that his attention was drawn to. Experiences such as these drove him to the point of suicide, but his art, in the last resort, prevented him, for he felt that he still had works to compose. Patience and resignation were the lessons that he had learnt, but he affirmed that he would go to meet Death joyfully. In the postscript there is a final outpouring; as the autumn leaves fall and wither, so his hopes of a cure fade. He leaves Heiligenstadt virtually in the same condition as he arrived: 'Oh Providence, grant me at least one day of pure joy – it is so long since the echo of real joy was in my heart – Oh when – oh when, Great God – shall I hear this echo again in the temple of nature and mankind – Never? – Oh, that would be too hard.'

And yet there had been days during that summer when he was inspired with 'high courage', and out of that summer came also the second symphony in D, Op. 36, which is a radiant work, full of vitality and felicities, bearing no hint of the spiritual crisis evinced by the Heiligenstadt Testament. Moreover, from the remaining correspondence for the year we find Beethoven in fighting spirit over the matter of pirated editions of his works, bantering with Zmeskall, specifying his requirements for pianos that the makers were now clamouring and vying with each other to make for him – in short on top form. He was also about to appear before the Viennese musical public in yet another guise, this time as a composer of oratorio.

The fact that Beethoven had decided to make a foray into the genre was indicated by his brother Caspar in a reply dated 23 November 1802 to the publisher Johann André of Offenbach-am-Main, who had written to enquire whether Beethoven had anything available for publication. In his reply Caspar referred to a symphony and a piano concerto, which would cost him 300 florins each, and three piano sonatas at the same price each, which would not be available all at once, however, but at intervals of five or six weeks, since the composer no longer troubled himself with such 'trifles', but composed only operas, oratorios, etc. It was made quite clear that there was absolutely no question of any discussion over the amount of the fee. Apart from the rather silly light in which Caspar revealed himself in the letter, it is interesting, nevertheless, that the name of Beethoven was now sufficient to call its own tune, and also that the composer was probably thinking of writing an oratorio. Certainly in the longer term this was true, for Beethoven was to move on to both oratorio and opera over the next year or so.

His chance soon came when he was approached by Emanuel Schikaneder (1751-1812), manager of the Theater an der Wien and author of *The Magic Flute*, to compose an opera, and this commission carried with it free lodgings in the theatre buildings. As early as 12 February 1803 Johann van Beethoven had made known, in a letter to Breitkopf & Härtel, the existence of the commission. The libretto was to be Schikaneder's *Vestas Feuer*. In the meantime, Beethoven's presence as house composer – along with Abbé Vogler – meant that he was able to obtain the use of the theatre, and on 23, 26 and 30 March 1803, it was announced that Herr Ludwig van Beethoven would produce his new oratorio on 5 April. The work in question was *Christus am Ölberge* (*The Mount of Olives*, as it is usually known in English), Op. 85, which Beethoven said he composed in a fortnight.

He seems to have been confident that the concert was going to be a success, for he doubled the prices of the front seats, tripled the prices of the reserved ones, and asked twelve ducats instead of the usual four florins for each box. Beethoven later denied this, and in a letter of September or October later that year to Breitkopf & Härtel he thanked Rochlitz, the editor of their *Musikalische Zeitung*, for publishing such a flattering report of the oratorio; but that the information about the prices was a blatant lie. Beethoven then wrote somewhat archly that he presumed that this was done to prove that the paper was impartial. By all means, he went on, if that is what helped to sell copies. In the event the performance was said to have made Beethoven the sum of 1,800 florins, and the audience certainly had their money's worth. In addition to the oratorio they heard the first and second symphonies and the piano concerto in C minor, Op. 37. Ferdinand Ries maintained that even more works had been envisaged, but because of the length of the concert they were omitted in performance. His account of the final rehearsal is well worth reading:

> The rehearsal began at eight o'clock in the morning. It was a terrible rehearsal, and by half-past two everybody was exhausted and pretty well dissatisfied. Prince Karl Lichnowsky, who was present at the rehearsal from the start, sent for bread and butter, cold meat and wine in large hampers. In a pleasant way he asked everybody to help themselves, which they did with both hands, so that good humour was once more restored. Then the prince asked that the oratorio be rehearsed once more, so that it might go well in the evening and Beethoven's first composition in this genre be presented in a worthy manner. So the rehearsal began again.

August von Kotzebue, writing in *Der Freimüthige*, said that although the two symphonies and parts of the oratorio were well received, the work as a whole was too long, too artificially constructed, and too lacking in expressiveness, especially in the vocal writing. The text, which was by F. X. Huber, seemed to Kotzebue as superficial as the music. Schindler maintained that in later years Beethoven agreed with much of the criticism, and certainly he felt that it had been a mistake to treat the part of Christ in the modern operatic manner of *recitativo accompagnato*. The verdict of posterity, in the

*Electoral splendour. An ante-room in the south wing
of the palace at Brühl.*

present century especially, has been largely to endorse this general opinion of the work. In spite of the oratorio's lack of success, however, Beethoven was not deterred from vocal writing, and was still writing an opera to a libretto by Schikaneder, according to *Die Zeitung für die Elegante Welt* of 2 August that year, though under the date of 29 June.

At this point the rather exotic character of George Polgren (or Polgreen) Bridgetower came into Beethoven's life. Bridgetower, or Brischdower, or Brischdauer, as the composer transliterated his name, was a mulatto violinist born in Poland in 1779 who made his way to England, where he became leader of the orchestra of the Prince of Wales (subsequently George IV) at the Brighton Pavilion. He obtained leave of absence to travel on the Continent, and was certainly in Vienna by 16 April, when Beethoven invited visitors to a musical gathering at Schuppanzigh's, where Bridgetower performed. Beethoven took to him and helped him by introducing him into Viennese society–even to some members of it that he did not actually know, as we see from a letter dated 18 May from Beethoven to Baron Wetzlar von Plankenstern:

> Despite the fact that we have never met, I have no hesitation in introducing to you the bearer of this letter, Herr Brischdower, a very capable virtuoso and a perfect master of his instrument. He not only plays his own concertos but is an excellent quartet player, too. I sincerely hope you will find him a greater circle of friends . . . I think it would be no bad thing if you took him to Therese Schönfeld one evening; they say many friends gather at her house, or if you were to invite him to your house . . .

We also know from other letters that Beethoven had Bridgetower invited to the Guicciardi house for dinner, and also Count von Deym's, and there must have been others of which no record remains.

As far as Beethoven's music is concerned, however, Bridgetower's chief interest lies in the fact that the *Kreutzer* sonata, Op. 47, was originally composed for him. Beethoven's dedication ran: 'Sonata mulattica. Composta per il Mulatto Brischdauer gran pazzo e compositore mulattico (Mulattick sonata. Composed for the mulatto Brischdauer, great madman and mulattick composer).' According to Bridgetower, the reason for the change in the dedication was that they fell out over a girl. Be that as it may, it seems obvious that Bridgetower had the sort of talent that pleased Beethoven through its sheer virtuoso quality, though it seems to have been a rather spontaneous and rather short-lived affair, and one may be permitted to infer that there was probably no very good basis for a more deep and lasting friendship.

E. Schikaneder (1751-1812), actor, dramatist and librettist, as well as theatre director. It was during his tenure of office as manager of the Theater an der Wien that Beethoven was commissioned to write an opera, though his choice–Schikaneder's Vestas Feuer*–was destined never to be completed.*

It is equally true to say, however, that the friendship with Kreutzer does not seem to have been all that deep either. He had come to Vienna in the spring of 1798 with Bernadotte, and his visit had given Beethoven a great deal of pleasure, according to a letter of 4 October 1804 to the publisher Simrock, and Beethoven admitted in this letter that he only wrote to Kreutzer once a year. Kreutzer's modesty and unaffected nature, unlike that of so many other virtuosi, obviously appealed to Beethoven. He was therefore anxious to hear from Simrock when the sonata was ready for publication, so that he could write Kreutzer a note about it. The original dedicatee, Bridgetower, was never referred to in the letter, except by inference, when Beethoven said that the sonata was written for a 'competent' violinist. We may leave the final word on the matter to Berlioz, who declared that Kreutzer: '. . . could never bring himself to play this outrageously unintelligible composition'.

Beethoven spent the summer of 1803 first in Baden, and then in the village of Oberdöbling outside Vienna. It was at this time that he began serious work on his third symphony, the *Eroica*, Op. 55, and he was certainly at work on it when he returned to Vienna that autumn to his rooms in the theatre, for it was there that Stephan von Breuning visited him, along with Willibrord Joseph Mähler, who made several likenesses of Beethoven. When asked to play something, Beethoven played the finale of his new symphony (according to Mähler) and then extemporised for a space of two hours. Since the work was not completed until May 1804, one wonders about the veracity of Mähler's assertion that it was the finale of the *Eroica* that he heard, though it was no doubt possible that it was sufficiently advanced by then for Beethoven to play a version of it to his visitors.

Beethoven's dealings with his publishers continued as before, though his circle was growing ever wider, and on 20 July George Thomson wrote to him from Edinburgh to ask him to compose accompaniments and instrumental obbligato parts *ad libitum* for the Scottish folksongs he collected. Beethoven agreed to this request, though it took him until 5 October to answer the letter, largely because of his absence in the country and also 'several very urgent occupations'. One of those urgent occupations was the *Eroica*, another was possibly his new pupil Archduke Rudolph, who started having lessons during the winter of 1803-04, and yet another was the opera that he was supposed to be writing for Schikaneder. As we learn from a letter of 2 November to the painter Alexander Macco, then in Prague, he had only just begun work on it, and it was supposed to be produced for the following Easter (1804).

As ever with Beethoven, however, nothing was ever certain for very long, especially in the field of human relationships. We learn from a letter of 4 January 1804 that Johann Friedrich Rochlitz had sent Beethoven the first act of a libretto for an opera, but the composer returned it on the grounds that the plot was concerned with magic, and magic was not box office in Vienna. However, if Rochlitz were to have another libretto up

The Theater an der Wien, c. 1815. It was in this theatre, on 22 December 1808, that the fifth and sixth symphonies were first heard, along with the Choral Fantasy, the piano concert in G, Op. 58, and movements from the Mass in C, Op. 86.

Above: The Archduke Maximilian Franz of Hapsburg arriving in Bonn as the new Elector and Archbishop of Cologne in 1780. From a painting by F. J. Roussaux.

Opposite: A contemporary chalk drawing showing coach travel towards the close of the eighteenth century. When Beethoven left Bonn for the second time to go to Vienna, he had no idea that he would never see his native city again, though he often contemplated returning there until very late in life.

Archduke Rudolph (1788-1831) in a miniature by J. B. Isabey. This Hapsburg prince became a pupil of Beethoven in the winter of 1803-04, and was the composer's consistent and generous patron.

his sleeve, complete, and without magic, then Beethoven would be delighted to have it, for just now he was in need of a text for an opera, because he had broken with Schikaneder. This, Beethoven maintained, had set him back fully six months, since Schikaneder had done nothing to improve his libretto which, despite its supposed Roman subject matter, contained language that Beethoven felt might be more suited to Viennese apple-women. In spite of the fact that he had already composed some of the numbers, Beethoven withdrew from the arrangement with Schikaneder, and took comfort from the fact that the latter's 'empire' had been entirely eclipsed by the light of the brilliant French opera. Beethoven could not close the letter without a shot at Rochlitz, in his capacity as editor of the *Allgemeine Musikalische Zeitung*, for some of the unfavourable things that had appeared in it about the composer. But he attributed this to ignorance of the facts of musical life in Vienna, and in particular the number of Beethoven's enemies there.

Probably the most important point to emerge from this letter, however, certainly as far as Beethoven's subsequent career is concerned, is that he had already had 'an old French libretto' adapted, and was then about to begin work on it. This was none other than J. N. Bouilly's *Léonore ou l'amour conjugal*, which had been translated and adapted by Joseph Sonnleithner for Beethoven. But the composer's joy at having finally found a libretto and being able to make a start on his opera was soon clouded over by an upheaval at the theatre. Bartholomäus Zitterbarth, having previously bought out Schikaneder's share in the Theater an der Wien, then sold it to Baron von Braun in February 1804. Schikaneder had subsequently been retained by Zitterbarth as director, but Baron von Braun dismissed him. The only good thing to emerge from this upheaval was that Sonnleithner, who had taken over from Kotzebue as secretary of the court theatres that month, acted as director of the Theater an der Wien, at Baron von Braun's request, as a temporary measure.

There is a letter in existence from Beethoven to Sonnleithner which probably dates from March 1804, in which he announced that he had decided to travel, and asked Sonnleithner to be sure and have the libretto finished by the middle of April, so that Beethoven could get on with the composition and the opera be produced

F. Ries (1784-1838), pianist and composer, in an engraved portrait by C. Mayer, c. 1825. Ries had had dealings with the Beethoven family since Bonn days, for his father Franz had been a colleague in the Electoral establishment. After studying with Beethoven, Ferdinand made several successful tours as a concert pianist, and then settled in London, where he did all that he could to help Beethoven, though often this was not to the master's liking.

in June at the latest. The composer evidently felt bitter about what he regarded as Baron von Braun's persistently unfriendly treatment of him, and one suspects that his threat to leave the theatre building or to travel was largely retaliatory: 'I shall never crawl. My world is the universe.' Apparently in the course of the transfer of ownership of the building, Beethoven's claims had been neglected, and he was most unhappy. Probably for this reason he took lodgings in the same house as Stephan von Breuning from roughly May to October that year, whilst still laying claim to his rooms in the theatre. At all events it was a far from satisfactory arrangement, and precipitated a most unfortunate quarrel with von Breuning.

Since it seemed silly that two friends of such long standing should occupy two completely separate apartments in the same house, Beethoven gave up his quarters and moved in with von Breuning. He was certainly the one who came off best, for von Breuning had a housekeeper and a cook, kept his table, and had a stable household. Beethoven's domestic life was almost the exact antithesis. He had got through three servants during the upset over the rooms at the theatre, and small wonder, since they had to sleep in the kitchen, 'apart from other inconveniences'–to quote Beethoven's own words on the matter. However, in vacating his quarters in the apartment building, which belonged to the Esterházy family, Beethoven neglected to give due notice, and suddenly found himself liable for the rent, despite the fact that he was no longer occupying the premises.

At the beginning of July the matter came up at dinner, and soon a most terrible altercation developed. Beethoven–unable to concede that he was capable of being in the wrong–took off for Baden, near Vienna, and accused everyone but himself. He held the long-suffering Ries responsible, and had said so during the course of the dinner, whereas Beethoven's brother, who had been present, thought that von Breuning was to blame for the fact that he was liable for the rent, and that this constituted a slur on his character. Von Breuning wrote to Beethoven, but the latter was adamant, and vowed that he would never speak to him again, and declared that he had known all along that things would take this turn. To make Beethoven's condition more uncomfortable, the weather at Baden was bad, and he found it difficult to protect himself against people. In a series of letters to Ries all of this was catalogued, and the charges against von Breuning heaped up. His brother had been slow in ordering the wine for him that he found so necessary for his health; he was going to have to find a new apartment in Vienna, and in the immediate future he wanted to leave Baden for Döbling, so Ries was to ask his brother to make the necessary arrangements. The last sentence of a group of four

R. Kreutzer (1766-1831) in an engraved portrait by C. T. Riedel and A. P. Vincent, c. 1800. The violin sonata, Op. 47, that bears his name was initially dedicated to the much more colourful character George Bridgetower, and it is more than likely that Kreutzer never actually played the work.

letters to Ries at this time reveals a somewhat strange attitude to the terrible affair, as if in some way there had to be a sacrifice before the creative genius would or could perform: 'If a burst of truly hard work follows, something really fine may well be the outcome.' Beethoven was not the only composer who has seemed to function in this way; but it seems especially heartless when the sacrificial victims are loyal and dedicated friends and colleagues.

A letter written from Vienna on 26 August 1804 to Breitkopf & Härtel listed the works the composer then had available. First was the oratorio *Christus am Ölberge*, which he had revised by this time; next was a new grand symphony, in fact the *Eroica*; then the triple concerto, Op. 56, and lastly three new piano sonatas, of which the first was the *Waldstein*, Op. 53, the second the sonata in F, Op. 54, and the third the *Appassionata*, Op. 57. As Beethoven pointed out, the idea of the triple concerto was indeed something new, but was somewhat overshadowed by the interest of the *Eroica*, which Beethoven felt would appeal to the musical public. He also said that the symphony was really entitled *Bonaparte*. We shall consider the question of the dedication of the *Eroica* in conjunction with its first public performance. It would seem, however, that a fair copy had been made by early May 1804.

Opposite: F. J. Haydn (1732-1809) in the portrait of 1792 by T. Hardy. Despite the initial encouragement Haydn gave to Beethoven, their lessons were not a success when the latter returned to Vienna, and although their relationship lasted until the death of Haydn, it was always somewhat strained in character.

Right: W. A. Mozart (1756-91) in an unfinished portrait by Lange. The period that Beethoven was in Vienna for his first visit in 1787 was a difficult one for Mozart; he could give little attention to the young visitor from Bonn, though he recognised that he was highly talented. Mozart died, a pauper, before Beethoven could return to the Austrian capital.

Below: The Graben in Vienna in the early nineteenth century, looking towards the Kohlmarkt. Beethoven lived for a time at no. 214.

The opening bars of the march from Beethoven's
Eroica *symphony—*Marcia funebre—*which was
revolutionary in its day from several points of view,
not least its great length.*

The autumn of 1804 saw Beethoven back in Vienna, and in October he moved into rooms on the fourth floor of Baron Pasqualati's house on the Mölkerbastei, where he continued to live on and off until 1815. In fact Pasqualati was reputed to have determined not to let the accommodation whenever Beethoven left, since he knew that he would be back. There was also a highly emotive reconciliation with Stephan von Breuning, sealed by the sending of a coloured miniature done the year before by Christian Horneman of Copenhagen. As in a much earlier letter to Eleonore von Breuning, Beethoven attributed the whole misunderstanding to the interference of other, unworthy, people, which it patently was not. Even so, the tone of the letter is deeply contrite, and it is much to von Breuning's credit that he was totally understanding. On 13 November he wrote to Wegeler, by now von Breuning's brother-in-law through his marriage to Eleonore, and showed that he made ample allowances for the difficulties Beethoven had to come to terms with and, despite the trials to himself, gave not a hint of holding any of it against Beethoven. The only regret he expressed was that his involvement with Beethoven made him neglectful of his loved ones back in Bonn. By this time the composer was back into the habit of eating at von Breuning's table every day.

In November the piano concerto in C minor, Op. 37, was published, though it had been composed in 1800, and the *Eroica* was performed privately at Prince Lobkowitz's in December, when the famous oboist, Ramm, from Munich, was on a visit to Vienna. However, the first truly public performance of the symphony took place on 7 April 1805, and although work had been completed earlier, as we have already seen, consideration of it rightly belongs here.

According to the writer in *Der Freimüthige* of 26 April 1805, reactions to the symphony tended to fall into one of three categories. First there were Beethoven's friends, who maintained that this was a masterpiece, and that if audiences did not find it particularly pleasing at the moment, it was because they were not yet sufficiently cultured, musically speaking, to understand it. Next were those who denied that the work had any artistic merit whatsoever. All they could see in the work were indications of an unrestrained attempt at being odd, through strange modulations and violent transitions.

In their view the true expression of genius lay in producing something that was both beautiful and sublime. Since, in their opinion, Beethoven had already shown himself capable of this, his most recent offering was little short of perverse. There was, however, a third group–very small–whose position was somewhere between the first two. As far as they were concerned the work contained many fine things, but was confused at times in its continuity, and they found the enormous length particularly hard to bear. If it was tiring for those who were well versed in such things, then it was unbearable for a simple music lover. Czerny said that one man shouted from the gallery: 'I will give another kreutzer [farthing] if only the thing will stop.'

Evidently Beethoven was making great demands on his followers and admirers, though in many ways this was only the beginning, and if the *Eroica* alone was to be the stumbling block, then the sheep would be separated from the goats very quickly. Indeed one feels a certain sympathy with the reviewer, who was of the opinion that the time might well come when only those who were initiated into the complexities of music would be able to enjoy it. Where would this leave the average concert goer? The answer was that if they could not go along with him, then Beethoven was happy to leave them behind. As the reviewer himself observed, neither the audience nor Beethoven was pleased with each other that evening. As far as the audience was concerned, the symphony was too long and too difficult– and the composer rude, for he did not even make any sign of acknowledgment to those members of the audience who were sufficiently enthusiastic to applaud him. The reviewer therefore assumed that, in Beethoven's opinion, they were not enthusiastic enough.

The *Allgemeine Musikalische Zeitung* registered a similar reaction, and though its reviewer professed himself one of Beethoven's sincerest admirers, he also found the work too long, and its more beautiful aspects ruined by what he could only regard as anarchy. At all events, Christoph Kuffner maintained that Beethoven had told him that of all his symphonies, the *Eroica* was the composer's favourite, and when taken to task about its inordinate length, the composer is said to have replied: 'If I write an hour-long symphony they will find it short enough.' Such was the degree of conviction held by Beethoven about his mission.

Needless to say, the inspiration and dedication of the work have had many words devoted to them, almost to the exclusion of any consideration of the music itself,

The Lobkowitz Palace in Vienna, where Beethoven's Eroica *symphony was heard privately before being presented to the world at large. Prince Franz von Lobkowitz was a violinist of some distinction, and maintained a private orchestra in his palace.*

59

*Top: A harpsichord of 1782, made by Burkat Shudi
and John Broadwood and now in the Victoria and
Albert Museum. At this period in music, the
harpsichord was rapidly losing ground to the piano.*

*Above: In 1798 Beethoven again visited Prague – he
had been there two years earlier – where he gave a
performance of the B flat piano concerto, Op. 19, and
possibly the one in C, Op. 15, also.*

*Opposite: Beethoven's study in Heiligenstadt. His
testament can be seen on his work table.*

and the traditions began very early on. Andreas Bertolini, for example, who was a doctor and assistant to Malfatti, through which he became a friend of Beethoven, told Otto Jahn in 1852 that it was Napoleon Bonaparte's expedition to Egypt that had first given the composer the idea of the *Eroica*, and that the funeral march (the second movement) was inspired by the rumour of Nelson's death at Aboukir. What seems much more likely was that the appointment of Jean-Baptiste Bernadotte as French Ambassador to Vienna in 1798, which also brought Kreutzer to the city, was a stimulating event for Beethoven, who at that time much admired Napoleon, First Consul of the Republic. Schindler even went so far as to say that the fair copy of the score, with its dedication of only two words – Napoleon Bonaparte – was ready for Bernadotte to take to Paris when the news reached Vienna that Napoleon had had himself proclaimed Emperor of the French, on 20 May 1804.

Ferdinand Ries, on the other hand, maintained that only one word – Buonaparte – was written on the title page of the score, with 'Luigi' van Beethoven at the bottom of the page, and since he was the person who brought the news to the composer, one is more inclined to accept his word. He recorded that Beethoven flew into a temper, and said: 'So he too is no other than an ordinary man. Now he will trample on all the rights of man, and simply gratify his ambition. Now he will set himself up like all the others and become a tyrant.' Beethoven then went to the table and tore off the title page. The work was then renamed *Sinfonia eroica*.

It is amusing to learn, a little later in this passage, that it was not only the mere music lovers who were taken unawares by the strangeness of the work. During the first rehearsal for one of its private performances in Prince Lobkowitz's palace prior to the first public performance, Ries felt that the horn player had come in at the wrong place, and said so to Beethoven, who was conducting. In fact the horn player had been right, it was Ries who was wrong, and he said that the composer did not forgive him for a long time. Still, Ries was used to that, having experienced Beethoven's wrath before.

The title page of the Eroica, *with the name of Bonaparte crossed out, and (opposite) the title page of the printed version in the collection of the Gesellschaft der Musikfreunde in Vienna, dedicated to Prince Lobkowitz, and subtitled 'to celebrate the memory of a great man'.*

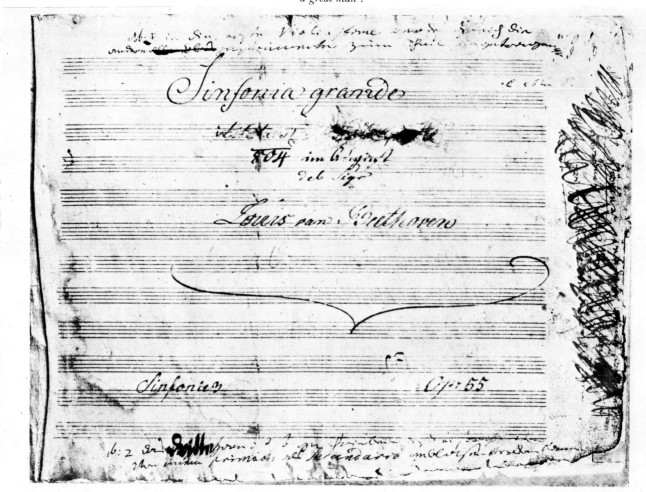

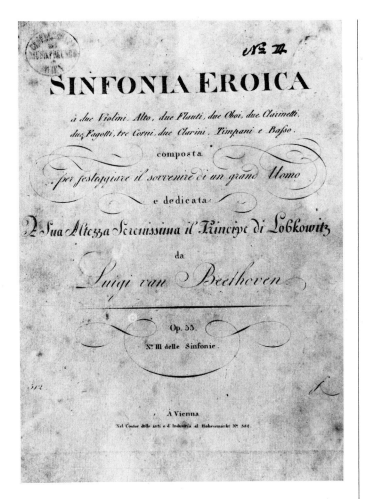

Perhaps we may leave the last word to Georg August Griesinger, who wrote in a letter to Breitkopf & Härtel, dated 13 February 1805:

> ... the symphony has been heard in concerts at Prince Lobkowitz's and at the house of a keen lover of music called Wirth, with singular applause. I hear that it is a work of genius, both from those who admire and those who denigrate Beethoven. Some maintain that it has more to it than the music of Haydn or Mozart, that the symphonic poem has been taken to new peaks.

In this he was more accurate than he could have possibly known, writing as he did before the public performance.

We learn from correspondence between Breitkopf & Härtel and Beethoven at this time that he was trying to interest the firm in the publication of both his oratorio and the *Eroica*, and had certainly sent them the score of the symphony by 16 January. On 18 April he again wrote to them, insisting that they publish the symphony in two months' time. As it turned out they did not publish it at all (the Bureau des Arts et d'Industrie did, in parts, in October 1806), and from a letter dated probably 21 June 1805, we learn that yet once more Beethoven had fallen out with publishers–this time over money–but a letter from Breitkopf & Härtel dated 30

January had only reached Beethoven the day before, which explains the delay over publication.

A more interesting aspect of the correspondence at this time is the number of letters to Countess Josephine von Deym, and their affectionate tone. Josephine (1779-1821) was the third child of Count Anatol von Brunsvik, and she married Count Joseph von Deym in 1779. She was left a widow in 1804, however, and until she left Vienna in 1808 with her two sons and her elder sister Therese, she and Beethoven were close friends. It would seem evident that the composer hoped to marry her, and that she had a considerable affection for him, though they were never on intimate terms, always addressing each other with the polite *Sie* and not *Du*. Later, in February 1810, Josephine married Baron Christoph von Stackelberg, and her sister Therese always felt that it was a great pity that she had refused Beethoven. She certainly felt that Josephine would have been happier with him than she was with von Stackelberg, but that in marrying the latter she had put the interests of her sons before her own desires. Beethoven's finances must still have been a cause of anxiety to him in the early years of her widowhood; however, in a draft of a letter to Beethoven, presumably written about this time, Josephine maintained that she was unable to respond to the sensual side of Beethoven's love for her. Obviously her recent bereavement might explain the need for a period of repose before involvement in emotional, and certainly physical, relationships, and she had in any case come to admire Beethoven through his music in the first place, rather than on an emotional, let alone a physical, plane. The transition to accepting him in his all too physical reality may have been too much for her, and the added question of his stability from a financial point of view, and therefore as a suitable second husband for herself and step-father for her two sons, may have persuaded her, somewhat reluctantly, to put herself at some distance from him.

The spontaneous outpourings from Beethoven that appear in these letters have led people to imagine that Josephine von Deym was the recipient of the letters to the 'Immortal Beloved', though current thinking on the matter tends to make Baroness Dorothea von Ertmann, a brilliant pianist, the most likely candidate, as we shall see in due course. If Josephine von Deym was not the Immortal Beloved, she nevertheless encouraged Beethoven a great deal in the spring of 1805 when he was working on his opera, and by the time he returned to Vienna in the autumn, after his usual summer migration, it was virtually completed. A letter to Joseph Sonnleithner written at this time says as much: 'I am completely ready now–and am awaiting the last four verses–I have already thought out the possible music for them–I definitely intend writing the overture in the course of rehearsals and only then.'

Above: Beethoven at the age of thirty-three, a year after he wrote the Heiligenstadt Testament. This miniature by Christian Horneman of 1803 is generally regarded as the first good portrait.

Right: This anonymous miniature on ivory of the Countess Giulietta Guicciardi was found amongst Beethoven's possessions after his death. She was only

seventeen when she became his pupil, and he fell deeply in love with her.

Below: Therese, Countess von Brunsvik in J. B. Lampi's portrait. Therese took piano lessons from Beethoven, and they developed a close friendship. Her sister Josephine, subsequently Countess von Deym, was closer to the composer's heart.

In all Beethoven was to write four overtures to his opera, and the one referred to was what we now know as *Leonore* No. 2. Strictly speaking one ought to call the first version of the opera *Leonore* also, but to avoid unnecessary confusion it will be referred to simply as *Fidelio* throughout. Ries did not hear this first version because Beethoven refused to let him remain in the company, which included Prince Lichnowsky, who were invited to his house to listen to the composer playing through the score. Despite Prince Lichnowsky's intervention, Beethoven remained adamant, and Ries was obliged subsequently to return to Bonn. There, under French rule, he was conscripted. Beethoven was unable to help him financially himself, so some time in September he gave Ries a letter to Princess Josephine von Liechtenstein, asking her to help Ries. He did not deliver the letter, however, but kept it as a proof of Beethoven's friendship for him. Ries spent most of the next three years in Paris in such depressing circumstances that he almost abandoned the idea of music as a profession.

In such unsettled times opera was hardly likely to be a flourishing concern, and the houses were thin. Then, on 13 November, the French entered Vienna. It was decided to give *Fidelio* on 20 November, only one week later. One cannot help but feel sympathy with the composer, as he struggled to put on his opera in such conditions. At the best of times it is a nerve-racking experience for a composer, but with the additional anxiety of the French invasion it must have been very difficult indeed. Friedrich Sebastian Mayer sang the part of Pizarro, and when confronted with a difficult passage retorted to the composer that Mozart, his 'brother-in-law', would not have written such damned nonsense. In fact Mozart was not, strictly speaking, his brother-in-law. He married the sister of Mozart's wife as her second husband. When one of the bassoon players was missing from a rehearsal, Prince Lobkowitz attempted to make Beethoven look on the brighter side of things, and said that he had two bassoonists already, so surely a third would scarcely be missed. This so enraged the composer that on his way home he yelled in at the front door of the prince's palace: 'Lobkowitzian ass!' Under the French occupation the palace became the headquarters of General Hulin; Murat took over that of the Archduke Albert, and Napoleon himself occupied Schönbrunn.

The opera ran for three successive nights, and in the circumstances it is hardly surprising that it was a flop. For one thing, the majority of such audiences as there were must have been Frenchmen, and any Viennese opera would have been hard put to arouse their enthusiasm, let alone one by Beethoven, whose own friends found adequate matter for criticism in the work as first performed. We have a most valuable account of what happened after that first run of performances from the tenor Joseph August Röckel, who related his experiences to Thayer in 1861. Towards the end of December a number of people, including Röckel, the newly appointed first tenor of the Theater an der Wien, were invited by Prince and Princess Karl Lichnowsky to their palace. Also present were Beethoven and his brother Caspar, Stephan von Breuning and Clement, leader of the orchestra at the theatre, along with four or five others.

The friends had decided amongst themselves beforehand what they thought that Beethoven ought to do to improve his opera, and not unnaturally faced the composer with a certain amount of apprehension. The whole opera was played through, according to Röckel, by Princess Lichnowsky at the piano, with Clement accompanying her on his violin in all the solos from memory, and Röckel singing as much of the music for high voice as he could; Mayer sang the low parts. The evening lasted from seven until one o'clock in the morning, and it was apparently only through the intervention of the princess that Beethoven was persuaded to omit three numbers. Naturally he protested and stormed, but by the time they all went off to supper, the composer was happier than anyone else present. One suspects that all the rest were far too exhausted to feel anything.

It must have been all the more frustrating to Beethoven that the French left Vienna again on 27 November, and the Peace of Pressburg was signed on 26 December that year. Had he been able to wait a little longer, his opera might have received better treatment. At all events, he set to work with a will, assisted by Stephan von Breuning, on a revised libretto of *Fidelio*. A letter to Sonnleithner, written by Beethoven in early March 1806, requested permission to continue to use his name in conjunction with the revised libretto. Basically, Beethoven wrote, the changes amounted to rewriting the first act, and reducing the original three acts to two.

Then, writing to Mayer at the beginning of April, Beethoven told him that Baron von Braun had threatened that if the opera was not given on Saturday 29 March there would be no further performances of it. Accordingly the work had been given in its revised form, and although the orchestra had not gone wrong, the singers had. There was to be one more performance of the work on 10 April, and another letter to Mayer, probably written on 8 April, two days before this performance, specifically asked Mayer to request Seyfried to conduct. The composer was somewhat wry about what he expected from the performance. He announced that he was going to listen to it from a distance, so that his patience would not be so tried, as it would be if he were too close, and had to listen to his music being

Part of Beethoven's autograph of Leb wohl du warmes Sonnelicht, *from his opera* Fidelio, *first given in unfavourable conditions in Vienna under French occupation, and much revised by the composer before he arrived at a satisfactory version.*

murdered. One might almost have thought that it was being done on purpose, he wrote. He refrained from mentioning the wind instruments, since they had been bad in the previous version of the work, and had been the occasion of his re-writing the overture (the new version was *Leonore* No. 3), all the dynamics had been removed in his opinion, and to hear his music performed in such a way left him with little desire to compose anything ever again.

There are basically two versions of why the opera failed to make its mark yet again. The first came from Stephan von Breuning in a letter of 2 June 1806 to his sister and brother-in-law, in which he stated that it was Beethoven's enemies who prevented any further performances. However, Röckel put forward a different version which, unlike that of von Breuning, was not coloured by close ties with Beethoven, nor was it motivated by any malice towards him. In his account he maintained that the opera had in fact been well received by the public, and that it would have become a favourite with them had not Beethoven himself prevented it. In an interview with Baron von Braun, Beethoven said he felt that he had been cheated out of his percentage of the takings. Von Braun pointed out that the houses were getting better, and would go on improving, until the galleries began to fill. To this Beethoven retorted that he did not write for the galleries.

Von Braun, however, replied that even Mozart did not think it beneath him to write for the galleries. It was not the comparison with Mozart that upset Beethoven, but the way in which von Braun, with a certain amount of justification, had reacted. The result was that the composer demanded his score back, von Braun rang the bell and ordered it to be fetched, and that was that.

Even if the detail of the ringing of the bell is an embellishment, we have a letter from Beethoven to Baron von Braun, dated 4 May 1806, asking for permission to borrow some of the orchestral parts in the theatre library so as to incorporate them in his own score, from which they had been omitted through lack of space. Prince Lobkowitz was, so Beethoven wrote, planning a private performance at his palace. We do not know whether this ever happened, but in the von Breuning letter of 2 June already referred to, he wrote that Prince Lobkowitz was sending the opera to the Queen of Prussia, and he hoped that performances in Berlin would make the Viennese sit up and take note. There were unfortunately no performances in Berlin at this time, however.

In the spring of this year Ludwig's brother Caspar married Johanna Theresa Reiss. So began a saga that was to cause the composer and all connected with him, whether as relatives or simply as friends, immense trouble until the composer's death. The fact that their son was born, according to the certificate of baptism, on 4 September 1806, would suggest that the marriage, on 25 May, had to take place. Even so, the wife brought her husband a dowry of 2,000 florins, and the house at Alservorstadt in which Caspar died was inherited by his wife from her father. At the time, however, despite the condition of the bride, there was nothing to suggest that the marriage would prove to be such a source of anxiety for the composer.

The day after the wedding, according to a note by Beethoven himself, he began the Razumovsky quartets, Op. 59, commissioned by the Russian prince whose name they bear, and from a letter to Breitkopf & Härtel dated 5 July we learn that he had already finished one of them. In a curiously perceptive interjection, he said that he was thinking of devoting himself almost completely to the *genre* of the quartet. In the eyes of some, he

Napoleon receiving the surrender of Vienna on 13 November 1805, an engraving by Stein of the painting by Girodet. It was only one week later that the opera Fidelio *received its first performance, with such disastrous results.*

67

Count (later Prince) A. Razumovsky (1757-1836), the extremely wealthy Russian Ambassador to Vienna who founded the famous string quartet that bore his name in 1808, and in whose palace (opposite)

frequent concerts were given. The quartet was virtually at Beethoven's disposal when he wished to have his chamber music performed.

carried it to one of its highest summits. In the same letter Beethoven also offered the G major piano concerto, Op. 58, dedicated to Archduke Rudolph. The comment by von Breuning in his letter of 2 June, that Beethoven was still suffering from the effects of his disappointment over the failure of his opera to the extent that he was having trouble in composing, had soon ceased to be true.

It does not seem as if Beethoven followed his usual summer habit of moving out into the country in 1806. Instead he went to Hungary to stay with Count von Brunsvik, and then to Silesia to stay with Prince Lichnowsky at his castle of Grätz, near Troppau. It was from there that he wrote to Breitkopf & Härtel on 3 September, offering now all three of the Razumovsky quartets, the fourth piano concerto, the fourth symphony, the score of *Fidelio* and *Christus am Ölberge*. We also have a letter to Count Razumovsky (as he then was) which may well date from this same period, and which was probably sent as a covering note with the second of the quartets, announcing that the third and last would soon be ready also.

Razumovsky was Russian Ambassador to Vienna, and in 1808 he was to establish his famous quartet of Schuppanzigh, Sina, Weiss and Linke, which existed until the Razumovsky Palace was burned down in 1814.

Of all his music, perhaps these quartets were least understood at first by Beethoven's contemporaries. Czerny said that when Schuppanzigh and his companions first played through the first quartet they laughed, and thought that Beethoven had played a joke on them, and that the music was not really meant to be the quartet that he had promised them. The violinist Felix Radicati, who said that he had fingered the string parts for Beethoven on the manuscript, was simply of the opinion that they were not music. To which Beethoven merely answered that they were not for Radicati, but for a future age. In the face of such reaction, Beethoven had need of a certain philosophical approach. It is interesting that on a page of one of the sketches he wrote: 'Let your deafness no longer be a secret – not even in art.'

Beethoven decided to stay on at Grätz that autumn, but his visit came to an abrupt end. Prince Karl Lichnowsky wanted him to play for the officers of the French army of occupation, and arranged a musical evening to that end. Beethoven, however, refused to play for them, despite several requests from the prince, and when it came to the evening in question, was nowhere to be found. A servant was sent to his room, but he had left the castle, leaving only a note for the prince, in which he said that he was unable to play for the enemies

Muzio Clementi (1752-1832), pianist and composer, and a music publisher in partnership with Collard in London. In the spring of 1807 he met Beethoven in Vienna, and his edition of the Emperor concerto, Op. 73, appeared before any on the Continent.

of his country. Despite the fact that it was dark, and pouring with rain, Beethoven went on foot to Troppau, clutching the manuscript of the *Appassionata* sonata. He had to spend the night there, and the following day had to enlist the aid of his abandoned host in procuring a passport for the return to Vienna. Beethoven is supposed to have written to Lichnowsky: 'Prince, what you are, you are by accident and birth. What I am, I am through myself. There have been, and will be, thousands of princes. There is only one Beethoven.'

Whatever the truth of the incident, the manuscript in the Paris Conservatoire is certainly stained with damp, and the walk through the night cannot have improved Beethoven's deafness, though it certainly did not cause it, as an old tradition maintained. As to the words to the prince, they may or may not have been those of Beethoven himself, but one thing is certain, and that is that the composer was well capable of having formulated them. In his defence, it was also mentioned that one of the French officers had asked him if he also played the violin, at which he took umbrage, and when he refused to play the piano there was a joking suggestion that he would be arrested, at which he took fright. Certainly at this time he was very sensitive to the apparently invincible progress of Napoleon. When he met Krumpholz in Vienna after the

Battle of Jena (14 October 1806) and asked him the news, Krumpholz told him of the French victory over the Prussians. Beethoven said angrily that it was a pity he did not understand the art of war as well as he understood the art of music, for then he would certainly defeat Napoleon.

Back in Vienna that winter, Beethoven was again in correspondence with George Thomson in Edinburgh and Breitkopf & Härtel in Leipzig, but perhaps the most important business before the end of 1806 was the first performance of the violin concerto, Op. 61, on 23 December at a benefit concert for Franz Clement, leader of the orchestra at the Theater an der Wien, for whom it was written. It was evidently written quite quickly, and Clement is supposed to have played the solo part at sight for the first performance. True or not, it is undoubtedly possible, in the way things tended to happen with Beethoven, though this does not prevent it from being one of his most beautiful works.

From the beginning of 1807 we have three letters from the composer to Marie Bigot and her husband, who was librarian to Count Razumovsky. Born at Colmar in Alsace, Marie Bigot became an excellent pianist, and came to Vienna with her husband in 1804. She went to Paris after only five years, where she became a piano teacher, and in 1818 gave lessons to Mendelssohn.

I. von Gleichenstein was an intimate friend of Beethoven, and was one of those responsible for drawing up the contract by which Archduke Rudolph, together with princes Lobkowitz and Kinsky guaranteed the composer an annual income.

When she played for Haydn on 20 February 1805, the composer was so moved that he told her it was not he who had written the music, but the pianist, and he wrote on the music that on that date he was happy. When Marie Bigot played one of Beethoven's sonatas to him, he remarked that her interpretation was not what he had envisaged, but that she was to carry on all the same, adding that if it was not exactly what he would have done, it was better. When the weather was fine that spring Beethoven suddenly invited Marie and her infant daughter to go for a drive with him, without Bigot himself being there. The invitation was refused, and Beethoven was at a loss to understand why, when his gesture had been inspired entirely by a spontaneous sense of exhilaration at the beautiful weather. It seemed at times as if there was some malevolent genius at work when it came to his relationships with other human beings.

On the other hand, a meeting with Muzio Clementi the following month turned out very well, and on 20 April Beethoven concluded an agreement with Clementi, on behalf of the publishing firm in which the latter and Collard were partners in London, for the publication of certain works by them, including an arrangement of the violin concerto for piano, which included an unusual cadenza for piano and timpani solo in the first movement. The letter that Clementi wrote to his partner Collard two days later is quite amusing for its tone:

> By a little management and without committing myself, I have at last made a compleat conquest of that haughty beauty, Beethoven, who first began at public places to grin and coquet with me, which of course I took care not to discourage; then slid into familiar chat, till meeting him by chance one day in the street–'Where do you lodge?' says he; 'I have not seen you this long while!'–upon which I gave him my address. Two days after I found on my table his card brought by himself, from the maid's description of his lovely form. This will do, thought I. Three days after that he calls again, and finds me at home. Conceive then the mutual ecstasy of such a meeting! I took pretty good care to improve it to our house's advantage, therefore, as soon as decency would allow, after praising very handsomely some of his compositions: 'Are you engaged with any publisher in London?'– 'No' says he. 'Suppose, then, that you prefer me?'–'With all my heart.' 'Done. What have you ready?'–'I'll bring you a list.' In short I agree with him to take in MSS. three quartets, a symphony, an overture and a concerto for the violin, which is beautiful, and which, at

L. Cherubini (1760-1842) visited Vienna in 1805-1806, and was warmly received by Haydn, amongst others, and was inspired to write a cantata on Haydn's death. But he had a very different reaction to Beethoven, with whom he found it difficult to form any association, though Beethoven admired his work.

> my request he will adapt for the pianoforte with and without the additional keys [the extra notes to give six octaves]; and a concerto for the pianoforte, for all which we are to pay him two hundred pounds sterling.

After this Beethoven had to write to Countess Josephine von Deym to ask her to write to her brother, Count Franz von Brunsvik, and let him have the Op. 59 quartets which Beethoven had left in Hungary. On 11 May, however, Beethoven wrote to the count himself with the same request. He evidently believed that the deal with Clementi was going to make him a lot of money, with good prospects for a continuing relationship. Unfortunately it did not work out that way, for Clementi remained on the Continent until 1810 with his pupil John Field, and Beethoven did not receive payment for three years. In the letter to Count von Brunsvik Beethoven also took the opportunity to suggest that he try to get the composer invited to give some concerts in Hungary, and if he did, then he would take his opera with him, since he would never be able to come to terms with the 'rabble' of princes who now ran the theatres.

This is a reference to the fact that on 1 January 1807 Baron von Braun had given up the management of the court theatres, which were now run by a consortium consisting of Princes Lobkowitz, Schwarzenberg and Esterházy, and Counts Esterházy, Lodron and Pálffy, Zichy and Nikolaus Esterházy. Acting on a hint from Prince Lobkowitz, Beethoven had drawn up a document in which he offered the new directors of the theatre – amongst other things – to compose a grand opera every year, along with an operetta, in return for a fixed remuneration and various other financial benefits. They either completely ignored this petition, or decided to do what they could for Beethoven individually. Certainly it was a difficult summer as far as finances were concerned, and the composer's health was not good either. He was at Baden in June, for which time there are a number of letters to Baron von Gleichenstein, mostly concerned with the follow-up to Beethoven's deal with Clementi. He offered the same works to Simrock in Bonn for Germany, Pleyel in Paris for France, and the Bureau des Arts et d'Industrie in Vienna for Austria.

Since Caspar Carl's marriage, Beethoven's other brother Nikolaus Johann, the chemist, was helping him in his dealings with publishers. However, on a date soon after 23 June, Beethoven wrote again to von Gleichenstein and told him to inform Nikolaus Johann that he (Beethoven) would never write to him again. The composer felt that he knew why his youngest brother was behaving badly. He had loaned Ludwig money, and was now worried that the composer would be unable to repay him. Ludwig, for his part, suspected that the two brothers were acting together in this matter, and that Nikolaus Johann was being encouraged by Caspar Carl. But in view of the fact that Beethoven's finances were chaotic at the best of times, Nikolaus Johann probably felt that if he were not paid back the money he was owed at a time when Beethoven was in funds, he might have to wait a very long time. He wanted to set up in business as a chemist on his own account, and therefore he needed the money which was, in any case, his. With a certain amount of ill grace Beethoven suggested in a letter to von Gleichenstein that he might as well draw the 1,500 florins from the Bureau des Arts et d'Industrie on the new contract, and so repay the debt. This presumably is what happened, for Nikolaus Johann bought the shop in Linz in a contract dated 13 March on the following year, 1808.

Another somewhat unfortunate incident happened in the autumn of 1807, arising from the Mass that had been commissioned the year before by Prince Nikolaus Esterházy for the name day of his wife, which fell on 8 September. Haydn had written six Masses for him after his return from London, and since he was no longer able to compose, Beethoven must have seemed the obvious choice. As the year advanced, the prince must have begun to wonder how the work was progressing, for the first performance was due on the Sunday following his wife's name day, which in 1807 was 13 September. So Beethoven replied from Baden on 26 July that in view of the fact that he had been unable to obtain the theatre for a benefit performance – a return to the 'rabble' of princes theme – he had been obliged to take advantage of offers from London (the Clementi contract), and so work on the Mass was held up. In addition Beethoven had been ill, and to prove it he enclosed a letter from his doctor because, he wrote, people were so quick to interpret everything he did to his disadvantage. Nevertheless, he promised the prince that he would have the work by 20 August.

The prince's reply, dated 9 August, was courteous and kindly. He was looking forward to hearing the work, and hoped that Beethoven was in better health. The composer went to Eisenstadt to conduct the performance, but it was far from a success. The prince wrote to a friend: 'Beethoven's Mass is intolerably stupid and horrible, and I am not certain that it can be performed properly at all. I am angry and mortified.' Not only was the prince mortified. The Kapellmeister at Eisenstadt was Hummel, and unfortunately Beethoven saw him laughing as he stood near the prince after the performance. The composer left the same day. It was probably not so much his pride that was hurt, though that must surely have been involved, but that a fellow musician of Hummel's standing should have been thought to react thus. In fact it would seem that Hummel was making fun of the prince for his reaction to the music, and was therefore on Beethoven's side.

On 20 September Beethoven wrote to Countess Josephine von Deym from Heiligenstadt, mentioning the visit to Eisenstadt, but giving no indication of what had transpired there. His deep affection for her was soon to be rudely hurt when she decided not to continue to see him, or at least to see much less of him than before. At first he could not really believe that she did not want to see him, but gradually he realised the truth, and his last letter to her ended on the same rather hopeless note as the relationship must have ended for Beethoven: 'You ask me to let you know how I am. It would not be possible to ask a more difficult question – and I prefer to let it go unanswered, rather than – answer it too truthfully . . .'

In 1809 a French diplomat, the Baron de Trémont, met Beethoven in Vienna. His attitude shows us what Beethoven's international standing was at this time, for in common with many other people outside of Austria, the baron admired Beethoven's genius, and claimed to know his works by heart. When he knew that he would be going to Vienna he asked Cherubini to give him a letter of introduction, but the latter said that there was little point. Haydn would make him welcome, but not Beethoven, and when Baron de Trémont approached Reicha with the same request, he pointed out that with Napoleon having just ordered the second bombardment of Vienna, he could hardly have chosen a worse time. Even so, the meeting took place, Beethoven was well disposed, and a friendship sprang up with the baron. Above all, it was Beethoven's piano playing that captivated his French friend.

When he felt inclined to improvisation . . . he was sublime. His tempestuous inspiration poured forth lovely melodies, and harmonies unsought because, mastered by musical emotion, he gave no thought to the search after effects that might have occurred to him with pen in hand; they were produced spontaneously without wanderings.

As a pianist, his playing was incorrect and his mode of fingering often faulty, whence it came that the quality of tone was neglected. But who could think of the pianist? He was absorbed in his thoughts, and his hands had to express them as best they might.

Baron de Trémont tried to persuade Beethoven to go to Paris with him, and at first the composer agreed to the idea. The mere thought of being able to show off such a prize catch to the musical world of Paris was sufficient to send the diplomat into raptures. The course of the war determined otherwise, however, for it took the baron away from Vienna, and by the time he returned, it was too late. However, this anticipates the story somewhat, for we must take up Beethoven's own business towards the New Year of 1808.

Part of the manuscript of the Sonata, Op. 57, Appassionata, now in the library of the Paris Conservatoire. The damp stains are believed to have resulted from Beethoven's walk through the rain clutching his composition after his refusal to play for the French at Grätz.

Heir to Mozart and Haydn

Beethoven in 1814, in a drawing by L. Letronne engraved by B. Höfel. In the opinion of Beethoven's contemporaries, this was one of the best likenesses of the composer ever to be made.

EARLY in 1808 Beethoven was still trying to obtain the Theater an der Wien for a benefit performance, and by now he had enlisted the aid of Heinrich Joseph von Collin, a poet and dramatist who had a post in the Imperial Finance Ministry. Von Collin was one of those who had been present when Beethoven's friends proposed revisions to *Fidelio* before its second appearance, and he was at this time trying to find a suitable libretto for the composer. The story of Bradamante, part of the *Orlando* epic, was mentioned as one possibility, though Shakespeare's *Macbeth* was also put forward. At all events Beethoven wanted to avoid magic, ballet and recitatives; he felt that these would detract from the impact of the work, as well as attract potentially unfavourable comparison with other, similar works that had been or would be performed. In this he was probably correct, though whether he had any justification for being quite so paranoic about the way he thought he was treated is open to doubt. The correspondence with von Collin continued throughout the year, and the poor man found himself drawn closely into Beethoven's attempt to have the theatre for his benefit.

This did not mean, however, that Beethoven had no means of putting on his music in public. During the winter of 1807-08, for example, there was a series of twenty concerts known as the Liebhaber concerts. At first they took place in the Mehlgrube Hall, and when this proved too small they were moved to the University Hall. Beethoven's second symphony was heard at the first concert; in November the *Prometheus* overture was performed; in December the *Eroica* symphony and *Coriolan* overture, and at the New Year the fourth symphony. This last work had also been heard on 15 November in the Burgtheater at a charity concert. Beethoven conducted many of these performances of his works, if not all of them. The series came to an end on 27 March 1808, and since it was Haydn's seventy-sixth birthday on the 31st, the last concert was given in his honour, with a performance of *The Creation*. Even after this, however, the *Eroica* was heard on 11 April at Sebastian Meier's annual benefit concert at the Theater an der Wien, and two days later, in a concert at the Burgtheater, the fourth symphony was played, together with a piano concerto, and the *Coriolan* overture, all conducted by the composer. In May the first recorded public performance of the triple concerto, Op. 56, took place in the Augartensaal.

Despite the fact that his music was being performed on what by any standards must be regarded as a fairly regular basis by now – for there must have been many private performances for music lovers of which we have no record – Beethoven was still talking of leaving Vienna, either for a tour in the winter, as he intimated in a letter to Breitkopf & Härtel at the beginning of June, or even for good. At all events he went to Heiligenstadt that summer as usual, and presumably it was there that he put the finishing touches to the *Pastoral* (Sixth) symphony. On his return to the city he moved lodgings, this time to the first-floor apartment of the Countess Erdödy in the Krugerstrasse, where Prince Lichnowsky lived on the second floor of the same house. The countess was yet another gifted pianist, who lived apart from her husband. Despite the fact that she was quite ill at the time, she gave a series of musical dinner parties which were greatly appreciated.

Sometime before 1 November, Beethoven received an invitation from Jérôme Bonaparte, brother of Napoleon and King of Westphalia, to go to Kassel as his Kapellmeister. The salary was to be 600 gold ducats per annum, and it must have seemed to Beethoven that at last someone had decided to give him the official recognition that he felt was his due, even if it did mean removing to a provincial town away from most of his friends. The fact that the invitation came from the brother, no less, of the hated Napoleon, shows how seriously Beethoven was contemplating leaving Vienna. The possibility that the Bonapartes might not have been destined to be in positions of authority for ever does not seem to have occurred to him.

There was another charity concert in the Theater an der Wien on 15 November, about which the details are not very clear, except that Beethoven conducted one of his symphonies and the *Coriolan* overture, and may even have been the soloist in one of his piano concertos. Joseph Hartl was the organiser of this concert, and it may well have been in recognition of this and the concert on 17 April that he gave Beethoven the theatre free for a concert in December. Hartl had been put in charge of the three theatres after the 'princely rabble' had had them for just one year – a year which had not been conspicuously successful, it would seem. At all events, the promised use of the theatre was something that Beethoven had long been trying for, and he made the best of it.

An advertisement in the *Wiener Zeitung* for 17 December announced that on Thursday, 22 December, Ludwig van Beethoven would hold a musical academy, in which all the pieces would be of his own composition, completely new, and not heard in public before. The programme was to consist of the *Pastoral* symphony, the aria *Ah, perfido!*, movements from the Mass for Princess Esterházy, the fourth piano concerto, Op. 58, the fifth symphony, a piano fantasia and the choral fantasia, Op. 80. This marathon performance, in which Beethoven played the solo in the piano concerto and the fantasia, was to begin at 6.30 p.m. Spohr was responsible for the story, told in his autobiography, that during the course of the performance Beethoven became so excited that he knocked the lamps off the piano. Two boys were then detailed to hold the lamps, but one came too close to Beethoven, who, excited once more, unintentionally hit the boy on the side of the head, whereupon he dropped his lamp. This may well have taken place at a rehearsal, however, rather than at a performance. The rehearsals themselves were marred by differences between Beethoven and the orchestra, so that Seyfried conducted, Beethoven remained out of sight in a side room with Röckel, and Seyfried came and consulted him from time to time.

When it came to the performance, things were hardly better. Anna Milder, who was to sing the aria, was offended by Beethoven and refused to perform, so Schuppanzigh's sister-in-law, a young and inexperi-

H. J. von Collin (1771-1811), the poet and dramatist who tried to find a suitable libretto for Beethoven to set to music, having also had a part in the revision of Fidelio *after its first unsatisfactory performances.*

enced singer, was brought in to replace her. When Beethoven, having brought her on to the platform, left her to begin the work, she was extremely nervous and did not perform at all well. Then in the choral fantasia there was some misunderstanding between Beethoven and the orchestra over whether a section was to be repeated or not, with the result that some made the repeat and others did not. In the ensuing chaos Beethoven stopped them and started again. Such a mishap was hardly likely to have endeared the composer to musicians who were already quite put out, and the fact that the concert lasted four hours can scarcely have improved their tempers. And yet the importance of this concert in the history of music cannot be underestimated. It was an amazing evening. It was also the last major occasion on which Beethoven performed in public as a solo pianist.

The fact of having at last been able to have the theatre for a concert and having had his new works performed, even if somewhat less satisfactorily than he would have liked, does not seem to have appeased Beethoven at all. On the contrary, it may even have convinced him that it was time to move on, and we find him writing to Breitkopf & Härtel on 7 January 1809 that he had accepted the offer to go to Kassel, and would pass through Leipzig on his way to take up his appointment: 'At last I have been forced, by intrigues, cabals and underhanded dealings of all sorts, to leave the only surviving German fatherland.' And in a postscript to the letter Beethoven suggested that something might be inserted into the *Musikalische Zeitung* – once his appointment in Kassel had been confirmed – to the effect that he was about to leave Vienna. A few acerbic remarks might also be included, since Beethoven was of the opinion that people in Vienna would never do anything for him that was worth mentioning. The last remark was not only unfair to those who had helped in many practical ways already, but was soon to be proved totally wrong.

When the news began to circulate that Beethoven was really thinking of leaving Vienna a group of his friends decided that they must do something to prevent him. The prime mover may well have been the Countess Erdödy, in whose apartment Beethoven was living at the time, in consultation with Baron von Gleichenstein. They must have been in close contact with Beethoven's pupil Archduke Rudolph, too, and the princes Lobkowitz and Kinsky, the three signatories of the contract that was eventually agreed with Beethoven on 1 March 1809. The most important factor was that Beethoven was to receive an annual income of 4,000 florins, payable in half-yearly instalments, for the rest of his life. In return he was to continue to reside in Vienna (or a city within Austrian territory), and travel only when necessary for business or in the interests of his art, and by prior consultation with the signatories. Other clauses contemplated by Beethoven, relative to an eventual imperial appointment and the right to the use of the Theater an der Wien on Palm Sunday each year for a benefit concert, were dropped, though it was specified in the final contract that if Beethoven received an official appointment at any time, then the income would cease if his salary was comparable. In a letter to von Gleichenstein, probably written about this time, Beethoven suggested that the three signatories might care to consider themselves part originators of each new work, for this would then leave no room for any impression that he was being paid a salary by them for doing nothing.

Within three days Beethoven wrote to Breitkopf & Härtel to tell them that his plans had changed, and that he was now going to stay in Vienna. Even so, he was still contemplating a short journey, depending on the state of the country. But with Napoleon once more advancing, this became increasingly less likely. Generally, however, Beethoven seems to have felt more at ease than perhaps at any time since he went to Vienna, and when writing to von Gleichenstein towards the middle of the month, he even suggested that his friend should find him a wife in Freiburg, where von Gleichenstein

then was. However, this euphoria did not prevent him from falling out with Countess Erdödy, the person who gave him shelter and had been instrumental in arranging the contract for the annuity. It is not clear exactly why they had the difference, but from a subsequent letter from Beethoven to Zmeskall it would seem that the countess had given his manservant twenty-five florins, and a further five florins each month, so that he would stay on with the composer and not leave him as so many others had done. Beethoven, already hypersensitive to the faintest suspicion of intrigue against him, and convinced that all servants were rogues, probably feared that his manservant would be encouraged to accept bribes from others, whose motives would be sinister, if not positively malevolent. Beethoven was suitably contrite and apologetic to the countess in a letter, but he later decided to leave her apartment. Thus were the efforts of his friends to smooth his path almost always rewarded.

The times were indeed troubled. As Napoleon advanced on Vienna the empress and the imperial family left on 4 May, and Archduke Rudolph went with them, occasioning Beethoven's inscription on the piano sonata, Op. 81a, *Les Adieux* (The Farewell). When the French arrived outside the capital they demanded that it be handed over, but Archduke Maximilian, who was in command, refused, and the city was shelled. Ries recorded that Beethoven went to the home of his

Prince Ferdinand Kinsky, one of the three signatories of the contract of 1809, whose death in 1812 created problems for Beethoven within three years of the salary being guaranteed. Prince Lobkowitz then died in 1816, but eventually both estates honoured the bond.

Louis Spohr (1784-1859), the German composer, was present when Fidelio, *revised, was presented in 1814. His memoirs contain a vivid description of Beethoven conducting.*

brother Caspar Carl, and during the bombardment went to the cellar where he covered his head with pillows so as to shut out the noise. Luckily the firing only lasted from 9 o'clock on the night of 11 May until 2.30 p.m. the next day, when the city surrendered. It was a particularly frustrating time for Beethoven. He was unable to get away to the country – certainly not for any length of time – probably until September, and in writing to Breitkopf & Härtel on 26 July, two weeks after the signing of the armistice, he said that he had hardly been able to do any work since the day in May when the imperial family left. Even so, he must have been composing the fifth piano concerto, Op. 73, the *Emperor*, at this time. The title, incidentally, was not his, and probably one of which he would not have approved at all, though it was dedicated to an imperial patron, the Archduke Rudolph.

There was a tragi-comic situation later in the year when Beethoven engaged a couple by the name of Herzog (German for Duke), to look after him, in the hopes that he would be able to eat at home and so save some money, but as ever he was no good at handling servants, and he had to resort to Zmeskall's aid in sorting things out when the latter returned to Vienna. Then he became ill, and it was in this state that he embarked on his fortieth year, and the new year of 1810. It was a period during which – in his own words – he worked for death rather than immortality. Things improved

slightly when Archduke Rudolph returned to Vienna on 30 January, and then early in February Beethoven heard that he might return to his old rooms in Baron Pasqualati's house.

The tone of his letters began to improve, and it was not only the effects of the spring that were responsible. Beethoven had fallen in love with Therese von Malfatti, niece of the famous Viennese doctor Giovanni von Malfatti, whose family came originally from Lucca. Suddenly the composer began to take an interest in his appearance once more. He borrowed a looking-glass from Zmeskall and asked him to buy one for him, since his was broken. He asked von Gleichenstein to buy shirts and neckcloths for him, and paid an advance on clothing to Joseph Lind, one of the best tailors in Vienna, on von Gleichenstein's advice. He was obviously hoping that Therese would respond to his affection. When he was with the von Malfattis he felt that he was among people who cared for him. He was happy, and felt that they would help to heal the wounds inflicted on his soul by wicked people. Then he had the inevitable hesitation. If he took down his mental barriers he would leave himself open once more to the risk of being hurt. Would it not be better, after all, to trust only to his own inner resources, and deliberately put from himself such potential sources of pain?

Other days found him in a much more positive frame of mind, however. For example, wishing to help Therese's mother to buy a new piano, since several manufacturers offered him special prices if he would use one of their instruments. He had not taken advantage of this hitherto. Then on 2 May he wrote to Franz Gerhard Wegeler in Coblenz, to ask him to procure for him a copy of his baptismal certificate.

But when von Gleichenstein became engaged to be married to Therese's sister Anna, Beethoven felt once more insecure. He told Zmeskall not to refer to him as a great man, because he had never been more aware of the strengths and weaknesses of human nature. He wrote to von Gleichenstein that he was either sailing on a calm sea, or had already entered a safe harbour, whereas he, Beethoven, was still struggling against the tempest. Beethoven suspected that von Gleichenstein knew something that he was either reluctant or afraid to tell the composer in case it hurt him. In such a situation Beethoven said that he would prefer to know, even if the news was disagreeable. His presentiment was probably correct, for Therese's family would not hear of her marrying Beethoven, and when he was turned down he subsequently broke off relations with them, and he was only reconciled with Dr von Malfatti on his deathbed.

In a letter written to Therese – the only one that has come down to us – about the time that he made the request for his baptismal certificate, he quoted some

The marriage of Jérôme Bonaparte, King of Westphalia (1784-1860), and Friederike Katharina of Württemberg. It was Jérôme Bonaparte's offer to Beethoven of a post as Kapellmeister at Kassel with a salary of 600 gold ducats which almost succeeded in luring the composer away from Vienna, to the dismay of his friends.

lines from Goethe's *Egmont*: 'People are not only united when they are together; the one who is far away, and even the departed, is present with us.' *Egmont* was much in his thoughts at this time, for it was first given on 24 May at the Burgtheater and again, with his incidental music, on 15 June. The words must have turned to ashes in his mouth, for no matter how much he might feel for Therese, the situation was hopeless, and no amount of holding her romantically in his thoughts could overcome the fact that he had been rejected. Even as all this was taking place, however, there was present in Vienna a person who was to be of immense help to Beethoven in getting over this blow, in the shape of Bettina Brentano.

This lively, if somewhat hysterical, lady from Frankfurt came into Beethoven's life through her half-brother Franz, who married Antonia, daughter of the collector, scholar and philosopher Joseph von Birkenstock, who lived in Vienna and had served both Maria-Theresa and Emperor Joseph. Unfortunately all that Bettina said and wrote about her relationship with Beethoven has to be treated with a certain amount of

care, and of the three letters which the composer is supposed to have written to her only one is widely accepted as being genuine. This autograph letter is dated 10 February 1811, when Bettina had gone to Berlin in preparation for her marriage the following month to Achim von Arnim. From this letter we can see how much Beethoven had enjoyed making Bettina's acquaintance, and how much he looked back with pleasure on a relationship that had begun in the previous May, for Bettina had written to Goethe, whom she had known since she was young, and told him of her having met Beethoven.

Apart from the sheer pleasure she brought to Beethoven after the disappointment over Therese von Malfatti, Bettina's chief importance in the Beethoven story is that she brought the composer into contact with Goethe sooner and more easily than might otherwise have happened. He told Bettina that he was about to write to Goethe on the subject of *Egmont*, though the letter in question was not written for another two months, and it was to be more than a year before the two men actually met.

Certainly Beethoven's outlook improved in the spring, for we find him going to concerts and, on 26 March, finishing the piano, violin and cello trio, Op. 97, in a matter of some three weeks. He had sketched it the year before. Moreover he wrote to Archduke Rudolph at this time about the trio and, reading between the lines – not that one has to look very closely,

however – one gets the impression that Beethoven was finding his obligations as the archduke's teacher somewhat irksome, in that they took him away from what he would much rather be doing; that is, pursuing his own musical bent. He had to cope with the constant problem of misprints in his works, too, which at this time seemed to be particularly bad. In fact he began a letter to Breitkopf & Härtel on 6 May with the words: 'Mistakes – mistakes – you yourselves are one huge mistake!' Then there was the eternal servant problem. In May he wrote a *cri de coeur* to Zmeskall that his servant was leaving that day, that he had no idea if and when the next one was coming, and would Zmeskall please send his servant round immediately, since Beethoven needed him for an hour. By this time word must surely have got around the employable of Vienna that here was one master who was to be avoided at all costs. It seems that Beethoven had a blind spot where servants were concerned, and he might almost be suspected of believing them to be a subhuman species, if somewhere above the animals. He showed some human sentiment, however, in a letter of 20 May to Breitkopf & Härtel, expressing condolences on the death of Härtel's wife, and musing that the inevitable parting of married couples in death was almost enough to put people off matrimony.

THERE IS evidence in this and other letters of the time that Beethoven was still looking for suitable operatic libretti, but von Collin, with whom he wished to work,

fell ill, and died on 28 July that year. It seems that Beethoven had found a suitable French melodrama called *Les Ruines de Babylone*, which Treitschke – though Ignaz Castelli was also involved in it – was going to adapt for him and then, in June, Beethoven discovered that it was intended to produce the original at the Theater auf der Wieden. In an outpouring of righteous indignation to Count Ferdinand Pálffy, administrator of the Burgtheater and a director of the opera, the composer maintained that he had rejected at least twelve possible libretti since the year before, and when at last he had encountered one that was suitable, and had made his intentions generally known, the ground was to be cut from under his feet. There is no evidence that Beethoven had started to compose the opera, but he appeared to be trying to give Pálffy that impression. Pálffy certainly must have co-operated to some extent, for in July the composer was able to send Treitschke the translation of the work which Pálffy had let him have, and Beethoven was keen that Treitschke should let him know soon whether or not he wanted to work with him.

Beethoven was getting ready to go to Teplitz (Teplice, now in Czechoslovakia) for the summer and was very keen that Count Franz von Brunsvik should go with him, otherwise he would be alone since his friend Franz Oliva was not there (Oliva had been the bearer of the letter from Beethoven to Goethe). Beethoven wrote to the count in June and again in early July saying that he would not accept a refusal. It all worked out well in the end, for although von Brunsvik did not go to Teplitz, he went as far as Vienna, and shortly after Beethoven's arrival in Teplitz, where he was to stay until 18 September, Oliva joined him.

At this time Beethoven had a commission to work on, *The Ruins of Athens*, Op. 113, which was to be the epilogue to the celebrations for the opening of the new theatre at Pest, due to take place on 4 October that year (1811). In fact it was then put off until 9 February 1812, when the prologue *King Stephan*, Op. 117, was also given. Even so, without some sort of society Beethoven's stay in Teplitz might have been boring for him, but he made the acquaintance of three people in particular who enlivened his time there. There were two

women, Amalie Sebald and Rahel Levin, and the latter's future husband Karl August Varnhagen von Ense, who recorded his impressions of the summer at Teplitz, which are of great value. For example, he expected to find the composer living up to his reputation as a wild and unsociable man, whereas in reality he turned out to have a heart of gold and a friendly disposition. He admitted that his deafness could make him an exhausting companion, and that Beethoven and Oliva had violent disagreements from time to time. By and large, however, the stay in Teplitz seems to have been a good one for Beethoven, for there were other friendships formed, particularly with Countess Elise von der Recke, and the poet Christoph August Tiedge. Another visitor was Prince Kinsky, whose contribution to Beethoven's annuity was in arrears. On 31 July 1810 the composer received what had been promised for the previous year and a quarter. Even so, the *Finanzpatent* issued by the Austrian government on 20 February 1811 had effectively reduced the value of banknotes to

Teplitz, the popular spa Beethoven visited in 1811.

K. A. Varnhagen von Ense and his future wife, Rahel Levin, whom Beethoven first met at Teplitz.

one-fifth of their original denomination. Archduke Rudolph gave orders for the necessary adjustment to be made when his portion of Beethoven's allowance was being paid, but Kinsky did not do so until a court decree on 13 September 1811, and in that same month Lobkowitz's payments were suspended for almost four years. When he took over the management of the court theatres his financial affairs had been thrown into a state of chaos, and his estates sequestrated. Beethoven's anxieties about finances were therefore not without justification. In the general air of austerity that prevailed in Vienna, theatres and concert halls did badly. Only charity concerts were at all patronised, since this was a way of helping those in distress.

Beethoven continued to compose through the winter, however, and on 23 or 24 May the next year (1812) he wrote to Breitkopf & Härtel that he was composing no less than three new symphonies, one of which was already finished. The first of these was the seventh, Op. 92, which according to the autograph score was completed on 13 May, and the second was the eighth, Op. 93. We must assume, therefore, that the third symphony was the ninth, Op. 125, though it was to be some time before composition began on it in earnest.

An incident that must have caused Beethoven pain at the time was not referred to in the letter, namely the reception at the first public performance of the fifth piano concerto, the *Emperor*, Op. 73. Composed in 1809, it was almost three years before it was first performed, on 11 February 1812. Beethoven was not the soloist, but entrusted the performance to Czerny. Even so the work failed to please, as Ignaz Castelli explained in his *Thalia*:

> If this composition . . . failed to receive the applause which it deserved, the reason is to be sought partly in the subjective character of the work, partly in the subjective nature of the listeners. Beethoven, full of proud confidence in himself, never writes for the multitude; he demands understanding and feeling, and because of the intentional difficulties, he can receive these only at the hands of the knowing, a majority of whom is not to be found on such occasions.

The summer of 1812 was again spent in Teplitz, and at last the meeting with Goethe took place. Beethoven probably arrived there on 5 July, having made a stop in Prague *en route* from Vienna. When Goethe, who arrived on 4 July, wrote to his wife two weeks later, he told her how struck he was with Beethoven's energy and intensity. He said that he fully understood how strange he must have seemed to the outside world. The next day, Goethe recorded in his diary, the two men went to Bilin together, and the following evening was spent at Beethoven's lodgings, where the composer played 'delightfully'. For a more considered appraisal of Beethoven by Goethe, however, we must turn to a letter he wrote on 2 September that year to Karl Friedrich Zelter. Beethoven's talent had amazed him, he wrote, but he described his personality as being unfortunately after his death on 26 March 1827. The letter was probably never sent, but naturally the identity of the intended recipient has caused much speculation. Countess Giulietta Guicciardi, Countess Therese von Brunsvik, Amalie Sebald and Countess Josephine von Stackelberg have all been suggested, and a current favourite is Dorothea, Baroness von Ertmann. Certainly she was one of the greatest performers of Beethoven's piano sonatas. He called her his Dorothea-Cäcilie, and the *Hammerklavier* sonata, Op. 101, was dedicated to her. Mendelssohn visited her in Milan in 1831 and she told him that after the death of her child, Beethoven could not bear to go and see her. Instead she eventually went to him. He sat down at the piano and said: 'We will now talk in music.' For over an hour he played to her and, in her own words, he said everything to her, and gave her consolation.

In the last resort, however, it matters little who the Immortal Beloved really was. If research, or the finding of a hitherto unknown document, proves her identity beyond doubt, that will not alter one word of the letter as it stands. Perhaps certain references would be clearer, but it would in no way alter the great candour and clarity with which Beethoven's personality is projected for us. Here is a man in his early forties, suffering a considerable physical disability, who knows that at

Amalie Sebald, the gifted singer whose friendship with Beethoven also dated from his visit to Teplitz.

intractable. Goethe could see that from Beethoven's point of view this was justified, since he found the world detestable, but at the same time he could also see that this did not make it any the more pleasant for himself or his friends. Of course Goethe felt that his deafness was largely responsible for this attitude, and for this Beethoven was to be pitied and forgiven. This affected the social side of his life more than the purely musical, and since Goethe felt that Beethoven was already a reserved person, he was sure that the deafness only served to increase the tendency. For Beethoven's part, whilst admiring Goethe enormously, he felt that he was too fond of court life. In the composer's opinion, this ill became a poet.

Something of which Goethe may not have been at all aware was that during this summer, in fact during that same month, Beethoven was once more emotionally involved, and all the evidence suggests that the letter in three parts written on 6 and 7 July to an unknown woman then at Karlsbad, is to be dated to 1812. The letter is usually described as being to the 'Immortal Beloved', though 'Eternally Beloved' would be more accurate. Be that as it may, the letter was found, together with the Heiligenstadt Testament and other documents, in a secret drawer in Beethoven's wardrobe

J. W. von Goethe (1749-1832), in a portrait by C. A. Schwerdgeburth. He and Beethoven met at Teplitz in 1812, and though the event was interesting for both men, it never resulted in any very lasting effect, let alone collaboration.

Bettina von Brentano, c. 1809, as seen by L. E. Grimm (1790-1863). Her vivaciousness pleased Beethoven, and she helped him get over his unfortunate love affair with Therese von Malfatti. She was also the means of bringing the composer and Goethe together.

his time of life he needs stability and security as enshrined in a love relationship and matrimony, who has already known disappointment and disillusionment, but who nevertheless tries to reach out yet once more to grasp the hand that is held out to him. That required no small amount of courage with a personality like Beethoven's, where there was so much at stake, so much to take hurt or harm. Indeed, this is exactly what may have happened, or the risk was too great, and the letter was kept back, never to be sent.

By 9 August Beethoven had gone, on the advice of his doctor, to Franzensbrunn, via Karlsbad, probably leaving Teplitz on 27 July. On 6 August he had played in a concert in Karlsbad in aid of the town of Baden, near Vienna, which had been almost completely destroyed by fire between 26 and 28 July. Almost 1,000 florins were raised at what must have been a rather thin and extemporary affair from Beethoven's own description of it in a letter to Archduke Rudolph. It was, he wrote, a poor concert for the poor. Beethoven then returned to Karlsbad on 7 September, and was back in Teplitz on 16 September. The doctor had come to the conclusion that Teplitz was, after all, the best place for his patient. Even so, when Beethoven got back he was far from well, as we learn from what is a delightful sequence of letters to Amalie Sebald. Although the composer tells her of the progress of his health, it lacks the bitterness that is so often evident in, for example, his letters to Breitkopf & Härtel, and his delight at finding her once more in Teplitz may well have helped him to get over his illness sooner. As he wrote to her: 'If only I were able to express my thoughts about my sickness

as precisely as I am able to express my thoughts in music, I could soon help myself.' But Amalie and her mother left Teplitz on 23 September to return to Berlin, and soon after Beethoven himself returned to Vienna, for at the beginning of October he went from the capital to Linz to visit his brother Johann, who had been living there for the last four-and-a-half years.

It seems as if this journey was undertaken on the spur of the moment, both from Beethoven's behaviour on his arrival, and from a short note to Baron von Gleichenstein before he left, asking the quickest and cheapest means of getting to Linz, and requesting exhaustive information on the matter. Johann rented part of his house in Linz to a Viennese doctor and his wife, and had fallen in love with the wife's sister, Therese Obermeyer, who came to live with them and, in the course of time with their landlord, in sin. It would seem that Ludwig got to hear about this, and came to Linz solely to prevent a marriage. He is said to have gone to the bishop, the civil authorities, and even the police, in order to try and break up the relationship. The only real effect of his visit, however, was to cause a violent scene with his brother, which can hardly have done Ludwig's health any good, and precipitate the marriage, which took place on 8 November 1812.

Somehow, in the midst of this domestic turbulence, Beethoven found time to complete the eighth symphony – at least it is marked Linz, October 1812 – and the three *Equali* for four trombones, of which Nos. 1 and 3, arranged by Seyfried, were eventually played at his own funeral, on 2 November. The next day Prince Kinsky died as the result of a fall from his horse near Prague, and Beethoven had the wearisome business of trying to ensure, first from the prince's widow, and then from his heirs, that the promised annuity would continue to be paid. Because of the condition of Lobkowitz's finances, as we have already seen, Beethoven received nothing from that source between 1 September 1811 until after 19 April 1815, and now he received nothing of the Kinsky portion between 3 November 1812 and 31 March 1815.

At the end of 1812 the French violinist Pierre Rode came to Vienna, and Beethoven wrote for him the sonata for violin and piano, Op. 96, which he performed accompanied by Archduke Rudolph at Prince Lobkowitz's on 29 December, and again on 7 January 1813, the day following Rode's first public concert in Vienna. From the number of letters extant in which Beethoven excuses himself from the archduke's because of illness, one wonders whether the illnesses were genuine, or merely 'diplomatic'. If genuine as far as Beethoven was concerned, then they may well have been psychosomatic, and indeed it was becoming increasingly difficult for Beethoven to view his attachment to the archduke as anything more than 'servitude'. On the other hand, as Beethoven realised full well, the archduke was at that moment the only one of the original trio who was actually in a position to pay him his share of the annuity. In February 1813 Beethoven renewed his application to Princess Kinsky for payment of his annuity, and in the course of the first letter dated 12 February mentioned that he had to support his sick brother and family. Caspar Carl was in fact dying of consumption, but survived until November 1815. However, on 12 April 1812 he obviously thought that he was going to die, and drew up a document in which he appointed Ludwig guardian of his son Karl in the event of his death. On this occasion he rallied, but this document was to be the source of much sorrow in the future.

Beethoven went to Baden on 27 May, and there he found a certain amount of solace amid nature, but the question of the annuity still nagged at him, and the uncertainty of the outcome of the war in Europe increased his feeling of insecurity. Then in July he was obliged to return to Vienna, which he loathed doing, in connection with the Lobkowitz and Kinsky affairs. On his return to Baden, Count Razumovsky arrived with his quartet, and this afforded him no little pleasure.

Meanwhile, far away in Spain, Wellington had won the Battle of Vittoria on 21 June. This seemingly unconnected incident was the occasion for one of the more curious episodes in Beethoven's life, and the means of making him a more popular composer than ever before. Johann Nepomuk Mälzel (1772-1838), inventor of the Mechanical Trumpeter, approached Beethoven for a suitable composition for his other invention, the Panharmonicon. This contraption, blown by bellows, incorporated the instruments then in use in military bands within a case, and was operated by a revolving cylinder, much on the same lines as a music box. For this Beethoven wrote a suitably martial piece entitled *The Battle of Vittoria* (also known as *Wellington's Victory*), with suggestions from Mälzel, and concluding with a fugue on *God save the King*. The two men had known each other previously, Mälzel had tried to make an ear trumpet for Beethoven, and they had even contemplated a trip to London together in the spring, but the state of Caspar Carl van Beethoven's health made this impossible for the composer, and Mälzel was busy with his exhibition *The Conflagration of Moscow*, inspired by Napoleon's invasion of Russia and his retreat from the burning city. When Beethoven returned to Vienna that autumn, neither he nor Mälzel was exactly well off, and news that preparations were beginning in October for two charity performances of Handel's *Timotheus* in the course of the following month, in aid of the widows and orphans of the Austrians and Bavarians who had been killed in the wars, gave Mälzel an inspiration.

Mälzel proposed that Beethoven should orchestrate his *Battle of Vittoria*, and make it the star attraction of a charity concert for the Austrians and Bavarians wounded at the Battle of Hanau. The idea was that this would then lead the way to one or two subsequent concerts, which would be for the benefit of Beethoven and Mälzel. Beethoven wrote to Archduke Rudolph to ask for his help in securing the University Hall, which was granted for 8 and 12 December. The placards announcing the first concert gave the programme. First came Beethoven's seventh symphony, then two marches—one by Dussek and the other by Pleyel—to be played by Mälzel's Mechanical Trumpeter with full orchestral accompaniment, and finally *Wellington's Victory*. Initially the battle piece was described as Mälzel's property, which it was, strictly speaking, but when Beethoven objected, it was described as having been composed 'out of friendship', for Mälzel's forthcoming visit to London. In fact Mälzel had a considerable hand in the shaping of the work, as well as having produced the idea in the first place. The success of the first concert induced the organisers to repeat it four days later, and in all more than 4,000 florins were raised for the charity in question.

Of course there were plenty of people who were appalled at the idea that Beethoven should prostitute his talent in this way. Tomaschek, for example, who heard the battle piece the following year, declared that it pained him to see a Beethoven, probably assigned the highest throne in the realm of music by Providence, now appearing amongst the crudest materialists. On the other hand, highly reputable musicians took part in the first two concerts, and they did so out of curiosity to see and play Beethoven's music, encouraged by the charitable nature of the concert itself, and persuaded by Mälzel's personality and charm, which by all accounts must have been considerable. Such distinguished musicians as Dragonetti, Meyerbeer, Romberg, Spohr, Schuppanzigh, Hummel, Moscheles and Salieri took part, and most of them evidently thought that the whole thing was a great frolic – even if the music itself was far from easy to play.

In his autobiography the tenor Franz Wild described one of the performances, which corroborates what Spohr wrote about it. Apparently Beethoven indulged in the most extraordinary movements whilst conducting. For *piano* passages he would crouch down behind the conductor's stand, and for *forte* passages he would grow and grow in stature or even leap into the air. He would shout to reinforce the *fortes*. At the *pianos*, however, it was quite likely that Beethoven would not be able to hear the orchestra, so simply went on beating time and had to calculate where they ought to have got to in the score. When he overlooked a pause, this had disastrous results, but according to Spohr it only happened in rehearsals.

Whatever the opinion of purely musical experts on the battle piece, it was nevertheless a watershed in Beethoven's career, for it firmly made him Vienna's composer, not only for those who always had supported him, but for those who now recognised him as such. If Tomaschek was right in his assertion that the composer himself thought the work a piece of folly, he nevertheless recorded for us that Beethoven liked it because it was the work with which he thoroughly thrashed the Viennese. After the two concerts Beethoven prepared a note of thanks for insertion in the *Wiener Zeitung*, in which almost everyone worthy of praise was given his due, especially Mälzel himself. Unfortunately it was never published, for by then the composer had fallen out with the inventor. Eventually this was to lead to protracted legal proceedings, and even though right was probably on Beethoven's side from a purely technical point of view, since the matter turned on whether the orchestral version was the same as the Panharmonicon one, it is hard to feel that in the circumstances Beethoven acted anything less than shabbily towards Mälzel. For legal technicalities apart, Beethoven surely owed recognition to Mälzel's flair and vision in projecting the whole idea in the first place, even apart from any specific part that he may have played in the music itself. After all, what successful artist today would begrudge a competent and satisfactory agent his fair percentage?

Beethoven was now on a rising wave, however, and on 31 December a notice appeared in the *Wiener Zietung* to the effect that the work would be given again in the Grosser Redoutensaal on 2 January – for his own benefit; Mälzel was to have no part in it. Without Mälzel and his Mechanical Trumpeter, however, something else had to be found to fill out the programme. At a meeting held before the end of December with Count Moritz Lichnowsky at the apartment of the producer and bass singer Karl Friedrich Weinmüller, it was decided to include items 6, 7 and 8 from *The Ruins of Athens*, Op. 113. The bass aria, item 7, was to be sung by Weinmüller, and was held to be particularly appropriate, since the bust of the emperor was made to appear. This, however, needed to be concealed until the appropriate moment, and was the subject of an amusing letter from Beethoven to Zmeskall on New Year's Day 1814 – the day before the concert – in which he was desperate for a curtain, a screen or a veil: 'Hangings!!!! Or the aria and I will be hanged tomorrow. I press you as warmly to my heart in the new year as I did in the old – with or without curtain.' Since the concert was largely the same programme as before, and the majority of the performers were still available, rehearsal time could be cut and expenses kept to a minimum. The concert was a great success and, according to the *Wiener Zeitung* of 9 January, several items had to be encored. On 24 January the same paper printed a note of thanks from the composer. This time no names were mentioned, and certainly not that of Mälzel.

The immediate outcome of this new success was a plan with Weinmüller and Saal to revive *Fidelio*. They had been granted a benefit performance at the court opera, and the choice of work was left to them. In view of the wave of patriotic feeling that was carrying Beethoven high, and the fact that no work then in the repertory would fill the house, *Fidelio* seemed the obvious choice. Beethoven had to ask Count Moritz Lichnowsky for his copy of the score since, characteristically, Beethoven could not remember where his was, and Treitschke was commissioned with the task of reworking Sonnleithner's libretto. After seeing his work, Beethoven wrote that he now felt more firmly resolved to rebuild the desolate ruins of the old castle that was *Fidelio*.

In the meantime Beethoven decided to put on another concert in the Grosser Redoutensaal, on 27 February. The programme consisted of the seventh and eighth symphonies, with the battle symphony as a finale, and between the first two works the trio *Tremate, empi, tremate*, Op. 116, for soprano, tenor and bass. Beethoven had actually begun it in 1801, but only completed it in this form in time for the performance. This second concert was also a success, and the battle piece had another airing on 25 March, along with the *Egmont* overture, at a concert which Beethoven conducted in the Kärntnerthor Theater for the theatrical

86

*Pages one and four of the three-part letter to the
Immortal Beloved, which Beethoven wrote from
Teplitz in July 1812. The letter was found,
together with the Heiligenstadt Testament, among his
effects after his death, so was presumably never sent.*

charity fund. Nor were these concerts the only things to take Beethoven away from his revision of *Fidelio*. He composed the final chorus, WoO. 94, to a *singspiel* written by Treitschke called *Gute nachricht*, which was given to celebrate the triumphal entry of the allied armies into Vienna on 11 April. It was repeated four times before the end of the month, then once in May, and twice in June.

Mälzel was still in Vienna, doubtless contemplating somewhat ruefully the success Beethoven had had with the battle piece. Beethoven paid him back fifty ducats that he owed him, and they met in the office of a lawyer to attempt to sort out the thorny problem of the music and the proposed trip to England. Beethoven proved so obdurate, however, that Mälzel did not even bother to attend the last appointment arranged for the two men.

He had in any case by this time obtained parts of the battle music, from which he created a score, and left for Munich, where he had it performed on 16 and 17 March. When the news reached Vienna in April, Beethoven was furious, immediately instituted proceedings against Mälzel, and then sent a copy of the battle piece to London to the Prince Regent–to whom he dedicated the work–in an attempt to prevent what he regarded as pirated performances. This proved to have been a waste of time, since Mälzel was unable to mount any concerts when he arrived in London, and the Prince Regent simply put the work into his library and did not even acknowledge its receipt.

Beethoven was busy with work on *Fidelio* from March until 15 May, and the first night of the revised version was fixed for 23 May at the Kärntnerthor Theater. He began to compose a new overture in E – the one now known as *Fidelio* – only a few days before the performance, but was unable to finish it on time. On this occasion the overture to *The Ruins of Athens* was performed instead, and the new overture was played at the second performance on 26 May. There was now no doubt but that the opera was a success, and it received further performances on 2, 4, 7 and 21 June. By then, however, Beethoven was beginning to get anxious about his benefit performance, which had been fixed for 18 July. If there were too many performances of the opera, there would be no audience left to go to Beethoven's night. He need not have worried, however, for it was as successful as he could have wished.

All this time Beethoven was still attempting to have the matter of the Kinsky and Lobkowitz contributions to his annuity resolved in some way or other. At times in his frustration he felt that any sort of resolution would be better than this interminable round of letters and legal consultations. His financial position was improving, however – he was given the sum of 4,000 florins in silver by the nobility at the Congress, for one thing – and he organised concerts to make more. The gift was invested in a bank as an inheritance for Karl. He announced in the *Wiener Zeitung* a concert for 20 November in the Grossen Redoutensaal, which was first postponed to 22, then 27, and finally took place on 29 of that month. The battle piece was performed, to-

A letter from Beethoven to N. von Zmeskall, whom he describes as Conte di Musica. *Von Zmeskall was a Hungarian diplomat who, like so many well-born people at this time, was also an accomplished musician, in his case he was a cellist. His friendship with the composer was one of the most enduring, and he managed to comfort Beethoven at the very end of his life with gifts and communications, even though Zmeskall himself was infirm.*

Beethoven may well have hoped to go to Teplitz again this summer, but in the end went to Baden, though he returned to Vienna from time to time, and as the allied sovereigns began to assemble for the Congress of Vienna towards the end of September, Beethoven returned to the city. The first opera to be performed in the presence of the dignitaries on 26 September was, of course, none other than *Fidelio*. More performances followed on 4 and 9 October – these the fifteenth and sixteenth. On 5 September Treitschke and Beethoven had sent the score to Prague, and on 21 November it received a performance there, conducted by Carl Maria von Weber.

gether with a symphony – actually the seventh – which the reviewer in the *Wiener Zeitung* declared to have been composed as a companion piece. Such was the popularity and standing of Beethoven's 'folly' at this time. There was also a new cantata, *Der glorreiche Augenblick* (The glorious moment), Op. 136, which was recognised almost universally as having an extremely mediocre text. The concert was repeated in the same hall on 2 December, though with less success, and again on 25 December, in a benefit for the hospital of St Mark, when the results were much better. It had been intended that Beethoven should then have a benefit concert for himself, or so he wrote to Archduke Rudolph, but this idea was abandoned after the last concert. He had envisaged writing something new for it, but that idea came to nothing in the event. In the same letter he also mentioned plans for a new opera, and when not wrestling with the continuing saga of his annuity, it was with that in mind that he embarked on the new year of 1815.

The opera was to be *Romulus*, to a libretto by Treitschke. Beethoven had told Archduke Rudolph about it in a letter written during the month of December, and there is a note extant to Treitschke which may be dated to January 1815, in which Beethoven said that he had actually started composing the work. However, the composer Johann Evangelist Fuss then put a notice in the *Allgemeine Musikalische Zeitung* to the effect that he had written a new opera entitled *Romulus und Remus* for the Theater an der Wien. Beethoven immediately set about trying to prevent Fuss's work from appearing. One of his courses of action was to appeal to von Schreyvogel, secretary to the court theatres, and he may have persuaded the directors to tell Fuss that Beethoven would have the priority; there may also have been some sort of financial arrangement. Certainly Fuss's work was subsequently mounted at Pressburg; Beethoven's, however, never saw the light of day. But the incident is instructive insofar as it reveals how much influence Beethoven now had.

What was perhaps of more material satisfaction and benefit to the composer at this time was the fact that the question of the contribution to the annuity by the Kinsky heirs was settled on 18 January at the *Landrechte*, or appropriate legal body, in Prague. Archduke Rudolph intervened, but Beethoven had also the assistance of a lawyer in Prague, Johann Kanka, and then latterly had given a power of attorney to Baron Pasqualati's younger brother Josef to collect the money, and act for him in whatever way necessary to expedite matters. This was followed by a settlement of the Lobkowitz affair on 19 April; in both cases arrears were paid, and subsequent payments continued to be made until Beethoven's death. Despite the fact that Lobkowitz's affairs had been put in order before the end of the previous year, he had not thought it appropriate to come to Vienna before the spring of 1815, or so he wrote in a letter to Archduke Rudolph dated 29 December 1814. He also said that he had heard the Prague performance of *Fidelio* under Weber on 21 November, and he was delighted that Beethoven was at last receiving the recognition that was his due.

That recognition was growing constantly. On 25 February 1814 Sir George Smart had given *The Mount of Olives* – as the work is known in English – at the Drury Lane Theatre in London, and the following year, on 10 February 1815, and in the same theatre, the battle

Some of the hearing aids with which Beethoven tried to improve his deafness. The inventor J. N. Mälzel (1772-1838), with whom he collaborated on The Battle of Vittoria *in 1813, also tried to make him an ear trumpet.*

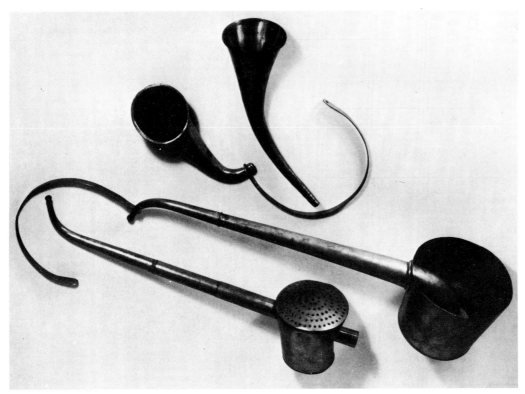

Sir George Smart (1776-1867), in a portrait by W. Bradley. A distinguished organist and conductor, Smart did much to bring Beethoven's music to the attention of the London musical public, though it was some ten years before he actually met Beethoven, when he went to Vienna in 1825.

piece was produced as the second half of the programme. It was Kramer, director of the Prince Regent's band, who showed the work to Smart, but Smart felt that it would not be suitable to end with a fugue on the National Anthem, so Ferdinand Ries added a short transitional passage at the end of the fugue, and the soloists and chorus joined in with the choral version of *God save the King*. Needless to say, the audience joined in too, it was repeated on 13 February, and with this and subsequent performances the work is said to have made Smart £1,000. The *Wiener Zeitung* reported the

performances on 2 March, which prompted Beethoven to contact Smart. In this he was facilitated by the fact that they had a mutual acquaintance in the Viennese businessman Johann Baptist von Häring, who was also an excellent violinist, and since he knew English very well he acted for Beethoven in his dealings on this occasion and subsequently with Thomson and others.

Then suddenly, out of the past almost, came the memory of Karl Amenda. A certain Count Keyserling had called on Beethoven in Vienna, and brought him news from Courland, which prompted the composer to write to Amenda on 12 April. This letter crossed with a package from Amenda, and a long letter dated 20 March, about an opera libretto by Rudolph von Berge entitled *Bacchus*. Beethoven may even have started writing some music to it, from evidence in the sketch books, but like so many of the ideas for another opera,

90

it never matured. About this time Beethoven was beginning to make plans for the summer, and at first toyed with the idea of going to Teplitz again, but he was influenced by the Erdödy family, who went to Jedlersee. When they left the area of the Schottenbastei in Vienna on this occasion, the Erdödys never returned to it. Lichnowsky, who had also lived there, was now dead, and Beethoven, with no friends in the neighbourhood, moved from the house Mölkerbastei.

Beethoven spent the summer and early autumn in Döbling, and much of the extant correspondence from this summer is with Countess Erdödy or her children's tutor Brauchle. There were pleasant musical occasions, and the principal compositions of this year, the two sonatas for piano and cello, Op. 102, were probably inspired by the fact that Linke, who had played the cello in the Razumovsky quartet, had been living with the Erdödy family since the burning of the Razumovsky Palace and the consequent disbanding of the quartet. After this idyllic period, the Erdödys then went to live on their estate in Croatia, and Beethoven never enjoyed their company in the same way again. There is evidence to suggest that eventually the Countess was banished for cruelty to one of her children, or even for poisoning, though this was such a common accusation in Vienna–Salieri was supposed to have poisoned Mozart–that perhaps one ought not pay too much attention to it. Looking back at that summer's correspondence, however, one can see–with the benefit of hindsight–that the clouds were gathering on the horizon, for Caspar Carl, Beethoven's brother, was rapidly getting worse, and when the composer returned to Vienna, probably in mid-October, his brother's life was drawing to a close.

There is a document in the Beethovenhaus in Bonn, dated 23 October 1815, in which Caspar Carl is refused leave of absence, and is ordered to return to work on 2 November. Pencilled on it, in Beethoven's writing, is the comment: 'This despicable result of financial officialdom caused my brother's death. He was in fact so ill that he was unable to fulfil the obligations of his situation without precipitating his death–a fine memorial supplied by those disgusting superior officials.' At about this time he wrote to Antonia Brentano in Frankfurt, telling her in the course of the letter that his brother had been retired on a pension. When he could not return to work on 2 November the bank retired him compulsorily, and he was in need of money. He possessed a pipe-bowl which, for some reason, he felt might be disposed of for the best price in Frankfurt. Beethoven was therefore asking Antonia to help him dispose of it, since many people came and went at her house, and Caspar Carl thought that his pipe-bowl would fetch ten *louis d'or*. Beethoven could not refuse him this request, he needed money to live, and life was precious to him, whereas for his part, Ludwig would gladly relinquish his.

Caspar Carl died on 15 November. The fifth clause of his will, dated the day before, had made Ludwig sole guardian of his son Karl, but a codicil of the same day intimates that Beethoven had already made it clear that he wanted sole *custody* of the boy, and the dying man could do little more than state that he wanted the mother and the uncle to have joint guardianship, and commend that his wife be compliant and his brother more moderate in the matter. In this way were sown the seeds of the tragedy that was to cloud the last years of the composer's existence.

Karl: Beethoven's Failure

BEETHOVEN took his newly acquired responsibilities towards his nephew very seriously; more than that, he was positively obsessive about him. Even given the fact that he did not approve of his sister-in-law, whom he referred to as the Queen of the Night, he never seems to have stopped to consider for one moment what possible harmful effects his determination to remove the child from her influence might have on the boy himself. In this matter, in his own estimation, Beethoven was right; his sister-in-law was not only wrong, but wicked into the bargain. His brother might have commended compliance to the wife and more moderation to his brother, but in so doing he was merely forecasting what would be the nature of their dealings in the future.

On 22 November the nine-year-old boy was put under the guardianship of his mother, and on 28 November Beethoven appealed to the Upper Austrian *Landrechte* to have the guardianship transferred to himself. The following day he was granted a hearing for 2 December, though when the day came it was postponed until 13 December. At the hearing Beethoven maintained that he could produce compelling reasons why his sister-in-law was unsuitable as a guardian, and on 15 December he was required to produce those reasons within three days, and if he did not do so, then the mother would be granted sole custody of the child. Beethoven did not even wait three days; on the very same day he brought what amounted to a charge of infidelity against his sister-in-law. There was an official communication on 21 December about the matter, but nothing was done during the Christmas and New Year holiday until 9 January 1816, when Beethoven was granted custody of the boy, and was required to present himself ten days later to take an oath and receive the order appointing him legal guardian.

This order also gave Beethoven the right to remove the child from his mother's care, which immediately posed a problem. His own household was far from suitable as an environment in which to bring up a young boy. It was therefore necessary to place him in a boarding school, and Beethoven chose one owned and run by Cajetan Giannatasio del Rio. Founded in 1798 in the centre of Vienna, the school was moved to the Landstrasse outside the city early in 1816. Even so, Beethoven had the idea from the very beginning that as soon as it was possible the boy ought to be moved away to a place where there was no possibility of his mother coming into contact with him. He wrote to Giannatasio del Rio on 1 February that he was bringing Karl the next day, and that he would arrange then the details as to how and when the mother was to have access to her child. One had to be on one's guard, he wrote, for she was not to be trusted. She had already bribed Beethoven's servant, and was obviously capable of anything.

In fact Beethoven had chosen well, since Giannatasio del Rio was married, and had two accomplished daughters, Fanny and Anna, who were both fond of music. Beethoven never doubted that he was acting in anything but the one true way, as we learn from a letter he wrote to Antonia Brentano in Frankfurt on 6 February. He saw himself as a knight on a white charger rescuing a child from the clutches of a worthless mother. He was in no doubt about the worries and cares that the child brought him but they were cares which, he maintained, were sweet to him.

Naturally Karl's mother was not inclined to accept this state of affairs without protest. She either appeared in person or sent someone to the school every day to remove the boy, and on 11 February the proprietor had to apply to Beethoven for formal authority to refuse the mother permission to take her son away. The composer took legal advice on the matter and appealed to the *Landrechte* for a formal statement giving him authority to exclude the mother or her agents from all direct contact with him. This was granted on 20 February, and in the meantime Beethoven wrote to Giannatasio del Rio about it, informing him that the Queen of the Night had been at the Artists' Ball until 3 a.m., exposing not only her intellectual, but physical nakedness, and it had been whispered that she was willing to hire herself for twenty florins. It was to such hands, Beethoven went on, that they were being asked to entrust their 'precious treasure'. He ended the letter by describing himself as Karl's father, and this was not just a figurative use of the term, for in a letter written later in the year to Kanka in Prague he took great pains, by his choice of words, to show that he regarded himself as the natural, bodily or actual father of the child since his own father's death: *wirklicher leiblicher Vater*. Beethoven even went so far as to confiscate a book that Karl's mother gave him in the course of a visit, and then decreed that she should only see the boy at Beethoven's house. In that way, he wrote to the headmaster, relations would be bound to be broken off much sooner.

In the meantime he was not neglecting his musical activities by any means. He had been commissioned to compose an oratorio for the recently formed *Gesellschaft der Musikfreunde*, and he was in communication with Birchall, the London publisher, as well as the Philharmonic Society in London. At one time and another Neate, Ries, Salomon and Smart all acted on his behalf, though largely through his own ineptitude in dealing with the society at this stage, and suspicion of the motives of individuals, who were in fact trying to do their best for Beethoven in a very difficult situation, the venture in London was not a success, either on the publishing front or with the society. They invited him to London much later, however, and encouraged him in the writing of the ninth symphony, as well as sending him £100 at the end of his life in recognition of his services to music.

With the break-up of the Razumovsky quartet, Schuppanzigh went to Russia and Linke to the Erdödys in Croatia, but before they went, they both gave farewell concerts. Schuppanzigh's was held on 11 February in Count Deym's palace, and the programme consisted entirely of works by Beethoven. In the quintet for piano and wind, Op. 16, the soloist was Carl Czerny, then in his mid-twenties, who took the liberty of adding some upper octaves to the piano part. Beethoven took exception to this, and told Czerny so in front of the others. The next day, however, the composer wrote to the

Nanette Streicher was the daughter of the piano maker Johann Andreas Stein. Her husband, Johann Streicher, was also a piano maker, and through mutual interest drew Beethoven to the family—this is a piano Nanette gave to the composer—Nanette did much to try and organise Beethoven's chaotic household when he was having difficulties with his nephew.

Carl Czerny (1791-1857), in a portrait by
J. Lanzedelly engraved by B. Höfel. The son of a
musician, Czerny became a fine pianist, a considerable
composer and a very successful teacher. His studies for
the piano are still widely used. Beethoven appreciated
his playing, but did not approve of the liberties
Czerny took on one occasion with his music.

Beethoven often went out of Vienna during the summer, especially to places that were then nearby villages such as Baden or Mödling, which is shown here.

pianist and apologised for his outburst. Beethoven explained that he would rather have his work played exactly as he had written it, however beautifully Czerny played it in his version. In the circumstances, that Beethoven was not only the composer but a pianist also, then Czerny accepted the rebuke. He had, after all, first taken lessons from Beethoven some fifteen years before this incident, and the composer had sufficient confidence in him to let him teach piano to his nephew whilst he was at Giannatasio del Rio's school.

Linke's concert was held a week later, on 18 February, at the *Römischer Kaiser* hotel, and again the programme was music by Beethoven, except for one work by Romberg. On 4 April Hummel left Vienna, only to reappear at Beethoven's death bed, and on the 20th Wild gave a farewell concert at which he sang *Adelaide* and *An die Hoffnung*, accompanied at the piano by the composer.

For some reason – possibly simply his obsessive attitude towards his nephew – Beethoven decided to take him away from the boarding school. In his letters in early May to Ries in London and Countess Erdödy,

then in Padua, he intimated that he was not satisfied with the arrangement, and on 28 July he wrote to Giannatasio del Rio that he intended to take Karl away at the end of the next quarter, by way of experiment. In the meantime Karl was to have an operation for a hernia – which eventually took place on 18 September – and during this period Karl's mother was to have even less access to him, since he would be all the more impressionable at such a time.

The next day the composer was due to leave for Baden, though he foresaw that he would have to go into Vienna frequently during his summer migration. In fact the operation was successful, Karl was well cared for by the headmaster's family, and they took him to Beethoven in Baden themselves. There, as Fanny recorded, Beethoven's mode of life in the country was exactly the same as in the city. He was forgetful of providing food for his guests, his rooms were in a permanent state of chaos, and he came to blows with his servant. This hardly augured well for the future of Karl when under the direct care of his uncle/father, and yet it was Beethoven's firm intention that on his return to

Vienna he would have a suitable household by some means. As usual in the matter of servants, the onus fell on Zmeskall, but things were evidently impossible by the beginning of November, and Beethoven had to write and tell Giannatasio del Rio that his household was like a shipwreck and would he please, therefore, keep Karl for another quarter.

Before the end of the year, Prince Lobkowitz died, on 16 December, so he never saw in print the dedication of *An die ferne Geliebte*, Op. 98, and a little cantata that Beethoven had composed for his birthday that month was never performed. Once again, Beethoven embarked on a new year, 1817, with a feeling of general unease. He had been ill in the autumn, and did not seem to be able to recover throughout the whole of the winter. Old friends had either died or left Vienna, and he was still thinking about travelling, though this might have endangered his annuity, and in any case he does not seem to have thought about what he would do with Karl. He hoped that travel would help his health, and might also help him to start composing again, for he had not written anything of importance for some time. Then at the end of April he moved house, so as to be nearer Giannatasio del Rio's school, and had the garden house there been suitable, he would have moved into it.

By the middle of May we find him at Heiligenstadt, having dispensed with the services of von Malfatti as his doctor in the previous month, and having concluded a contract with Karl's mother on 10 May for the financing of the boy's education and board and lodging. A letter to Countess Erdödy dated 19 June shows that he was still at Heiligenstadt, and contemplating a visit to her with Karl when his holidays began at the end of August. He also went into a long and intricate account of his illness and the treatment he was receiving for it. Early in July, however, he left Heiligenstadt for Nussdorf, where he remained until the middle of October, and it was probably there that he received a letter from Ries in London, written on behalf of the Philharmonic Society, in which he offered 300 guineas for Beethoven to go to London the following winter, write two symphonies for the society, and not accept engagements for any other major orchestral London concerts, or compose works for them, before or during the Philharmonic season (which would run from the end of February to the middle of June), without the consent of the society. He was able to give as many concerts for himself as he wished, and appear with other orchestras after the first two Philharmonic concerts, and was asked to be in London by 8 January 1818, and the society was willing to advance 100 guineas for the journey. Beethoven's reply, dated 9 July, was carefully considered, and in principle he was delighted with the prospect. He asked for the 100 guineas advance to be

given in addition to the 300 already offered, and of this 400, he wanted 150 to be given as an advance. The society refused this counter offer, though Beethoven did not have their reply until September, when he promptly accepted their first offer. However, he did not begin to write the two new symphonies – the ninth and tenth – which he would have to do, so as to be ready for London in January.

Meanwhile the Queen of the Night was making life difficult for Beethoven once more, and causing misunderstandings between the composer and Giannatasio del Rio, though as we have seen on many previous occasions, with Beethoven this was no very difficult thing to do. Another person became closely involved with Beethoven's domestic saga at this point, namely Nanette, the wife of Johann Streicher the piano maker, and daughter of the famous piano maker Johann Andreas Stein of Augsburg. She had known Beethoven for some time, but was only drawn closely into his private life at about the time that Karl became his consuming care.

On 1 November 1817, Beethoven wrote to Giannatasio del Rio to inform him that he was taking Karl away from the school at the end of the quarter – i.e. the end of January 1818, but that if his financial situation improved before then, he would let the headmaster know at the beginning of January. Giannatasio del Rio countered with an offer to keep Karl on for a reduced fee, but on 6 January 1818 Beethoven wrote to confirm the previous letter, despite the kind offer. Moreover it is clear from a letter written probably at the same time to Nanette Streicher that Beethoven still entertained ideas of having Karl to live with him. Indeed, one has the impression that Beethoven was using the financial question as an excuse, for from the letters to Nanette Streicher he had clearly intended to have a tutor for Karl who would live in the family, and that he would go to England later in the year. He wanted to keep the boy away from people whom he regarded as commonplace, and therefore put Nanette in a rather awkward situation. If she met the Giannatasio del Rios at Czerny's, she was to feign ignorance of Beethoven's plans for Karl. Moreover, Beethoven had not the courage to go in person to the school on the day Karl left – 24 January 1818 – but sent a letter of thanks instead.

This love of intrigue and secrecy is particularly evident in the correspondence with Nanette Streicher, and reveals a somewhat unattractive side of his nature. Largely with Nanette's help he had engaged two female servants – Nanni and Baberl – after his return to Vienna the previous autumn, but he was convinced that they cheated him and spied on him, read his letters, and were immoral. He considered them as beasts, and treated them as such. Books, utensils, even a chair were hurled at them – not to mention the torrent of words

The Esterházy palace at Eisenstadt.

Beethoven in 1818 in a chalk and charcoal drawing made by C. F. A. von Klöber at Mödling in that year, probably in preparation for a much larger painting, which is now lost, of the composer and his nephew.

poured on them. But there was worse than this. In an undated letter of 1817, which could date from before the women were engaged, or after he had taken them into his employ and therefore had enough of them, he asked Zmeskall if he could find him a manservant who could also do some tailoring. It did not matter, Beethoven went on, if he was somewhat hunchback, for Beethoven would then be able to use this as a weak point on which to apply pressure to the man. Was it any wonder, therefore, that with such an attitude of mind, Beethoven found it difficult to keep servants. Nanette found herself being appealed to as some kind of umpire – though of course expected to decide always in favour of Beethoven – in his squabbles with the servants, and she was expected to verify the housekeeping book, deal with the laundry, give advice about the purchase of table silver, and tell him whether he ought to drink tea after taking his emetic powder.

With such concerns, little composition was done. However, one event that stirred Beethoven's mind to the intent to do so, if it did not produce any very tangible result, was the despatch of a Broadwood piano on 27 December 1817 from London, as a gift from the maker. It did not arrive for some time, since it had to be shipped via Trieste, but Beethoven wrote a letter of thanks on 3 February 1818 in anticipation. It may have been this contact with London – or more probably a letter from Ries–that jogged Beethoven's conscience about the Philharmonic Society, for on 5 March he wrote to Ries in London to apologise for not having been able to go to England during the winter, but he hoped to be able to do so in the future. His health was one of the chief reasons cited, and indeed he arranged this year to go to Mödling, where he arrived on 19 May. What ought to have been another spur to composition was a commission from the *Gesellschaft der Musikfreunde* in Vienna for an oratorio on an heroic theme. An initial approach had been made through Zmeskall in 1815, but no more seems to have come of it, doubtless because of the problems encountered in setting up the *Gesellschaft* and getting it into operation. Beethoven replied on this occasion in 1818 that he only had a subject for a sacred theme, but all the same entertained the idea.

As ever, domestic matters were no better in Mödling than they had been in Vienna, and Nanette Streicher received a long letter on 18 June, informing her of how Beethoven's servants had been guilty of collaborating with the Queen of the Night, so he had dismissed them. Whilst they were in Mödling, Karl had been having some lessons from the village priest, but he, too, had aroused Beethoven's wrath. The saga continued through July, and in August Beethoven had to take Karl into Vienna for entrance examinations to the *Akademisches Gymnasium*. He can hardly have prepared for such examinations in less favourable conditions. Even more stress was to be put on the boy, for the following month his mother petitioned the *Landrechte* of Lower Austria to take from Beethoven the right to decide on Karl's future education. Her appeal was dismissed on 18 September, but three days later she made

application to have her son placed in a state institution, and she and Beethoven were ordered to appear before the magistrate on 23 September; Beethoven was to take a report on the boy's examination papers with him. The hearing was then postponed until 30 September. On 3 October the mother's appeal was rejected, and Beethoven emerged as the victor in that round. The boy went to school during November, friendly relations continued with the Giannatasio del Rio family, and it seemed as if all was well.

Then suddenly Karl ran away to his mother, early in December, and Beethoven was beside himself. He had to enlist the aid of the police to get him back, and he then placed the boy temporarily with Giannatasio del Rio. At a subsequent court hearing on 11 December, Karl's mother had the support of Jakob Hotschevar, a court secretary and relative through marriage. Their case made the well-being of the boy and his education the main concern, and in this context the disordered state of Beethoven's home and his deafness–two points on which he was most sensitive–obviously worked against him. A third factor was the question of his title to nobility. Whether he had deliberately misled the court in the first place or not, the fact of the matter was that the *Landrechte* was the competent body for matters relating to the nobility. They had assumed that the 'van' in Beethoven's name was equivalent to the German 'von', and as such an indication of noble status. Beethoven was unable to furnish any proof of nobility, however, for the simple reason that he had none. It was therefore obvious that the *Landrechte* was not the competent body, so on 18 December the matter was handed over to the *Magistrat der Stadt Wien*. Meanwhile Karl

The obverse and reverse of the gold medal, designed by Gayrard, sent to Beethoven by King Louis XVIII.

Opposite top: The University Hall in Vienna. The occasion depicted is the last concert given in Haydn's honour in 1808 when The Creation *was performed. Beethoven's audiences grew so large that his concerts of 1807-08 were moved here from the smaller Mehlgrube Hall.*

Above: Beethoven as painted by J. W. Mähler probably in August 1815.

Opposite, bottom: The old Burgtheater in Vienna in the Michaelerplatz, where Beethoven first appeared in public in the city, thus breaking out of the world of the aristocratic musical salons. Initially, however, he was still considered a virtuoso pianist rather than a composer.

The ninth symphony, for which Beethoven may have begun sketches as early as 1818, shown here in the composer's own hand. It is touching that his old friend Zmeskall attended the first performance in 1824, despite the fact that he had to be taken in a sedan chair in order to do so.

was with Giannatasio del Rio still, though kept apart from the other boys in the first instance.

So the year drew to its close, and few of Beethoven's intimates, let alone the composer himself, can have been sorry to see the end of it. Against this catalogue of woe, however, must be set the fact that Beethoven had completed, or made sketches for, three major works, namely the piano sonata in B flat, Op. 106, the ninth symphony, Op. 125, and the *Missa Solemnis*, Op. 123.

On 7 January 1819 the magistrates fixed a hearing for 11 January, which was to be attended by Beethoven, Karl, his mother and Jakob Hotschevar. Unfortunately we do not know the substance of what took place, though Fanny Giannatasio del Rio had recorded in her diary under the day before–i.e. 10 January–that Beethoven had had the guardianship of Karl taken away from him. In fact he was only temporarily suspended, and he still was technically responsible for the boy's education, though subsequently he voluntarily resigned the guardianship for a time, which was probably a wise move, since the magistrates may well have recommended this in any case. In response to that hearing on 11 January, Beethoven produced a letter or report, dated 1 February 1819, which ran to twelve pages, in which he elaborated his views on Karl's education. At this time Karl was attending an institution run by Joseph Kudlich, and spent some of the time with his mother.

When Beethoven resigned the guardianship on 26 March, Matthias von Tuscher was appointed in his stead, though with certain misgivings, and indeed he asked to be relieved of the task on 5 July. Meanwhile, sometime in May, Beethoven had appealed to Archduke Rudolph, to use his influence with his brother the Archduke Ludwig, to support Beethoven in his attempt to have Karl removed as far as possible from his mother's influence. In fact Beethoven was thinking of sending Karl out of the country at this point, to Landshut University in Bavaria. He was also ready to leave for Mödling for the summer, and arrived there on 12 May, so it was imperative that the matter be settled. When he was thwarted in his attempt, Beethoven then made application once more to Giannatasio del Rio, but the latter felt–probably quite rightly–that to take Karl back into his school again with the attendant risk of being caught in the crossfire between mother and uncle, could do the institution nothing but harm, and he declined. The family actually went out to Mödling on 17 June, according to Fanny's diary, to tell Beethoven so, and in the circumstances he then had to look elsewhere, and chose a school run by Joseph Blöchlinger. Karl entered it on 22 June 1819, and stayed there until 29 August 1823, so for a time that matter at least was settled, and the boy had some continuity of education, even if the war between his relatives still raged round him.

It had been known since mid-1818 that Archduke Rudolph was to be given ecclesiastical preferment, but this did not take place until 1819. On 24 April he was made a cardinal, and on 4 June Archbishop of Olmütz. The official announcement, and Beethoven's letter of congratulation, confirmed and affirmed, to the archduke, Beethoven's intention to write a Mass for him. Certainly the idea had been in Beethoven's mind, at least since he had known about the preferment in the previous year. Even when he was able to work on it that summer, however, his peace was interrupted by the resignation of Tuscher, the interim guardian, at the beginning of July, when he again acted as if he were sole guardian. He had in any case been considering himself as such the month before. By now his brother Johann was involved in the tug-of-war, since he had suggested that Karl should become a chemist like himself. Since Johann was obviously quite well off by now – it was during the course of this summer that he bought his estate at Gneixendorf – Beethoven's suspicious mind

professed the belief that his brother was able to bribe people. At the beginning of August he learned that his sister-in-law had proposed Johann as guardian to the magistrates, and during that month and into September he bombarded Blöchlinger with letters about Karl and his school regime, ending with orders on 14 September as to who the boy was to see, all in an attempt to keep his mother away.

We have a vivid impression of Beethoven at the end of August this year (1819), left by Anton Schindler, who visited him at Mödling with Johann Horzalka, a Viennese musician. They arrived about four in the afternoon, to find that Beethoven's two female servants had left that morning, and the whole house had been disturbed by a dreadful uproar in the Beethoven apartment that had taken place after midnight. The servants had had to wait so long for their master that they had fallen asleep and the food had been ruined. Beethoven was to be heard in the background, singing and stamping as he wrestled with the fugue of the Credo in the *Missa Solemnis*. The two visitors listened for some time and viewed the scene with alarm, so decided to leave, but just as they were about to do so the door of the inner

The fashionable promenade in the Prater, the park presented to the people of Vienna in 1766 by Joseph II.

Above: A nineteenth-century set design for a production of Fidelio. *The dungeon scene of Act II. Theatermuseum, Munich.*

Left: One of the numerous houses where the restless Beethoven made a temporary home. This is no. 2 Pfarrplatz, in Grinzing, now a suburb of Vienna.

Opposite: The Archduke Rudolph as the Archbishop of Olmütz, which he became in 1819. It was for him that Beethoven completed the great Missa Solemnis.

*F. Grillparzer (1791-1872), in a watercolour by
M. M. Daffinger, painted in 1827. Grillparzer first
met Beethoven in 1804 or 1805, but it was not until
much later that he attempted to collaborate with
Beethoven on the libretto for a new opera.*

room opened, and Beethoven appeared with such distorted features that he gave cause for alarm. As Schindler put it, he looked as if he had just come out of a struggle to the death with a whole army of contrapuntalists. As was often the case, Beethoven was cross when he realised that people had been eavesdropping, but he calmed down, and told the two men that he had had nothing to eat for over twenty-four hours, his servants had left him, and he did not know how he was to manage. Schindler helped him to dress, whilst Horzalka went off to arrange a meal at the restaurant of the nearby spa.

On 17 September the court gave the guardianship to the boy's mother, to be assisted by Leopold Nüssbock, a kind of municipal trustee. Naturally Beethoven protested, at the end of October when he returned to

Vienna, but on 4 November his appeal was turned down, and he was referred back to the decision of 17 September. He therefore decided to appeal to the Imperial and Royal Court of Appeal of Lower Austria, and the relevant material dates from January of the following year (1820).

Beethoven filed his petition with the Court of Appeal on 7 January and that court requested all the relevant material from the Vienna Magistracy, which duly complied, on 5 February, and referred to its decision of 17 September. Beethoven was greatly helped at this time by Johann Baptist Bach and Joseph Karl Bernard, and drew up his long memorandum of 18 February for the Court of Appeal. Possibly as a result of this, and the fact that Beethoven contacted two of the judges, Winter and Schmerling, the Court of Appeal requested a much fuller report from the Magistracy, which it presented on 28 February, and the commission which followed took place on 29 March. Beethoven refused to relinquish his rights, but requested Karl Peters, a tutor in the house of Prince Lobkowitz, as his associate guardian. Finally, on 8

April, the court pronounced its decision in Beethoven's favour. Karl's mother then appealed to the emperor – the only course left open to her – but he upheld the court's ruling. This was finally communicated to the interested parties on 24 July. As far as Beethoven was concerned, however, the matter was really over on 8 April, as he wrote to Karl Pinterics, private secretary to Count Ferdinand Pálffy: '. . . Dr Bach acted on my behalf in this matter; and this brook [a pun on the German word *bach*, which means brook] was joined by the ocean with thunder, lightning and tempest. The vessel of the Magistrat was completely shipwrecked there.'

Doubtless as a result of all the time and emotional energy Beethoven had to devote to this litigation, the Mass was not finished in time for the archduke's enthronement as archbishop on 20 March. Beethoven had hoped that it would be, and in correspondence with the Simrocks in Bonn at this time, when there was talk of a collected edition of his works, Beethoven had expected that the work would be ready 'soon'. He went to Mödling on 1 May, and remained there until the end of October.

Although the law case had been settled, Karl was still to cause his uncle trouble. He remained at Blöchlinger's establishment, though did not do particularly well, and when he was to attend an oral examination in June, he ran away to his mother. He was fetched back yet once more, and in view of the fact that Beethoven was advised that he would be unlikely to get a legal document to forbid her access to the boy, it was decided that the mother would not be admitted to the school, and would see Karl only at Beethoven's apartment. Since she was by no means keen to meet her brother-in-law, this would have the effect of reducing her interviews with her son considerably, though there would be clandestine correspondence and meetings, no doubt, as everyone more or less expected.

The winter of 1820-21 was not especially productive, for one thing Beethoven suffered from rheumatism, and illness continued to trouble him. By the first week of June 1821 he was once more at Döbling or Unterdöbling, as the letters of 18 and 19 July to the archduke indicate. By then it was obvious that he had contracted jaundice, and the doctor advised him to go to Baden. He therefore left on 7 September, and stayed in Baden until the end of October. The effect of the cure was that it brought on such violent diarrhoea that Beethoven dashed back to Vienna. In writing to Franz Brentano in Frankfurt on 12 November, he hoped that he had now regained his health, and that he would be embarking on a new life devoted to his art, after what he saw as a barren period that had lasted for the previous two years. He had written some 'pot-boilers' as he himself called them, which may refer to such works as the

Beethoven again visited Mödling in 1819, and whilst he was there working on the Missa Solemnis, *Anton Schindler visited him and found him in his usual state of domestic chaos.*

G. A. Rossini (1792-1868) was the son of an abattoir inspector who was also the town trumpeter. In 1821 he spent four months in Vienna, by which time he enjoyed a reputation throughout Europe, much to Beethoven's disgust.

Left: Carl Holz (1798-1858), was a talented amateur violinist whose irreverent and cheerful nature greatly appealed to the ageing Beethoven.

Below: The monument erected to Beethoven in 1888, when his remains were placed alongside those of Schubert in the Zentral-friedhof of Vienna.

Right: The bronze statue of Beethoven by Kaspar Zumbusch dates from 1880 and stands in the Beethoven-platz, Vienna.

Below: A living room on the first floor of the Beethovenhaus in Bonn.

bagatelles for piano, Op. 119, and he was obviously pinning great hopes on the future of the *Missa Solemnis*. In another to Franz Brentano, dated 20 December 1821, he implied that it was virtually ready for despatch. But the truth of the matter was that Beethoven was as we shall see not only playing one publisher off against another, but he was unashamedly using the friendship of Brentano, from whom he had borrowed money, into the bargain.

Early in May 1822 Beethoven went to Oberdöbling, where he remained until 1 September, and then went to Baden for about six weeks, returning to Vienna in mid-October. A letter to his brother Johann, written in May, shows that he was trying to arrange a rapprochement with his remaining family, and in fact during the following winter of 1822-23 Johann and Ludwig had rooms in adjacent houses in Vienna. His postscript to this letter expresses a wish that we have no reason for doubting was heartfelt: 'Peace, may we have peace. God grant that the most natural tie, that between brothers, be not broken again in an unnatural manner. At all events, my life will not last much longer . . .'

This sombre thought persisted in a letter to Carl Friedrich Peters, the Leipzig music publisher. Once more the idea of the collected edition of his works was in Beethoven's mind, so that he could oversee this 'during his lifetime'. Peters, however, like the other publishers, was encouraged to keep the matter of their dealings a secret. From a musical point of view, one of the more interesting things to come out of the correspondence with Peters in the summer of 1822 was that Beethoven was working on the first of the late quartets, Op. 127, subsequently completed to a commission from Prince Galitzin.

However, publishers cannot wait for ever, and on 13 May 1822, Simrock wrote to Beethoven to remind him that it was more than a year since the composer had promised to let him have the score of the Mass. Moreover, since 25 October 1821 100 *louis d'or* had been on deposit for Beethoven in Frankfurt. Simrock continued to hope that the Mass would arrive, and then on 13 September Beethoven wrote to him from Baden to the effect that since at least four other publishers had offered him the greater sum of 1,000 florins for the Mass, that was the price he would now have to pay to secure it. Simrock did not secure the Mass, and we do not know what counter proposal, if any, he made to Beethoven. It is possible that he agreed to accept something else in lieu of it, however, for the following year, on 10 March, Beethoven wrote to Simrock to say that he now had *two* Masses ready, but had not decided which Simrock was to have. He was in fact planning a Mass in C sharp minor, which he never composed, and had used the same excuse to Peters in Leipzig on 22 November 1822, though at least in that letter he had

had the grace to say that only one – the *Missa Solemnis* – was actually finished by then, and that the other one was not. When Peters too became impatient, Beethoven wrote to him on 20 March 1823, ten days after his letter to Simrock, and told him that he now had a third Mass projected! And this was after he had explored the possibility of publishing the Mass himself by subscription in January, February and March of 1823. On 19 March 1823, Beethoven finally presented a copy of the Mass to Archduke Rudolph. Three days later he wrote to Ries in London that within a fortnight he would finish the ninth symphony, Op. 125.

It was perhaps merely coincidence, but on 6 March Beethoven had suddenly written to his friend Johann Baptist Bach, who had helped him over the litigation in connection with the guardianship of his nephew Karl, that death might come at any time, and that he had not time at that moment to make a legal will. He therefore asked Bach to ensure that Karl was his sole heir and, as the executor, to find a guardian – provided that it was not his brother Johann. In particular Beethoven then referred to the seven remaining bank shares (there had been eight at first), which he regarded as some sort of sacred trust for Karl.

The publisher A. Diabelli (1781-1858), seen here in a lithograph by J. Kriehüber dating from 1841, was also a composer, though Beethoven described the waltz on which he wrote his Diabelli Variations as a 'cobbler's patch'.

The next month, in a period when it was more the tendency for old friends to die, or pass out of Beethoven's immediate circle, one actually returned to Vienna, namely the violinist Ignaz Schuppanzigh, who had settled in St Petersburg after the disbanding of the Razumovsky quartet after the fire which destroyed the Razumovsky Palace. On 26 April Beethoven sent him a canon by way of welcome, mostly to the word Falstaff or the Viennese dimunitive Falstafferel – a reference to Schuppanzigh's size. Then there was a deepening of a friendship with the poet Franz Grillparzer (1791-1872) who had first met Beethoven in 1804 or 1805 at the house of his uncle, Joseph Sonnleithner. The success of the revival of *Fidelio* had induced the theatre management to offer Beethoven a commission for a new opera. Lichnowsky had already told Beethoven in February that he was going to talk to Grillparzer, probably about *Macbeth* or *Romeo and Juliet*. Then, according to Grillparzer, Count Dietrichstein approached him, too,

Wilhelmine Schröder-Devrient (1804-60). The great singer made her debut in Mozart's The Magic Flute *as Pamina in 1821, and in the November of the following year, in spite of her youth, sang the part of Leonore in the successful revival of Beethoven's* Fidelio. *Indeed, she did much to make the work popular, and Richard Wagner had a great admiration for her.*

about a libretto for Beethoven. At first Grillparzer was hesitant; he was well aware of his lack of experience as a librettist; he also doubted Beethoven's ability to compose an opera at this stage in his career.

Eventually, however, Grillparzer decided on a subject from Bohemian legend, *Dragomira*, which he canvassed among Beethoven's friends before submitting to the composer himself. They all felt that it was suitable, though in the event it was changed for another subject, *Melusine*. What was more important at this stage, however, was the fact that the contact had been established,

The foyer of the restored Vienna State Opera – the
building was destroyed during the Second World War.
The celebrated house was reopened in 1955 with,
fittingly, a new production of Fidelio.

Beethoven was confident of being able to work with Grillparzer, and the will had been stirred. They met several times, and Grillparzer has left us a long account of the visit he made to Beethoven's apartment in the Kothgasse in Vienna, shortly before the composer left for Hetzendorf on 17 May. Beethoven was in a somewhat untidy bed in a nightgown that was far from clean. When the maid came in with butter and eggs, Beethoven seemed to Grillparzer to be devouring them instantly with his eyes before he had even tasted them, which gave the poet the impression that Beethoven's household was far from regulated. The composer said that he was going to the country in a few days, and would start to compose it as soon as he got there. Grillparzer promised to visit him once he had settled in at Hetzendorf, where Beethoven had been offered – and had accepted – the beautiful Villa Pronay belonging to a Hungarian nobleman Count Sigismund von Pronay Tót Próna und zu Blathnitza, also known as Baron Müller.

Grillparzer's meeting with Beethoven at Hetzendorf was of interest because in one of the conversation books used then the poet seems to have had an idea that looked forward to Wagnerian methods of composition by suggesting that *Melusine* might have a motif, which could be played every time she appeared, and used in the overture. As with other projects taken up by Beethoven, *Melusine* was destined never to see the light of day. One work which did, however, was the set of variations for piano, Op. 120, on a waltz by Diabelli, known as the Diabelli Variations. The *Wiener Zeitung* announced their publication by Diabelli on 16 June 1823, and in view of the time that they took to engrave and proof correct, it would seem almost certain that they were finished before Beethoven went to Hetzendorf. As with a great deal of Beethoven's career, the genesis of this work is the source of a good deal of legend. Basically it is safe to say that Antonio Diabelli, the music publisher, wrote a waltz and then had the idea of asking some of the most famous composers of the day to write one variation each on it, which he would then publish. Beethoven eventually wrote no less than thirty-three variations on what he referred to as Diabelli's 'cobbler's patch' (*schusterfleck*).

A NEW ILLNESS or affliction added itself to those already suffered by Beethoven during the summer of 1823, for he started having trouble with his eyes. In letters to Schindler, who had for some time now been acting as his factotum, and the Archduke Rudolph, there are references to this problem. Then Schlemmer, his old and trusted copyist, died this summer. But life was not all gloom. On 17 July he was able to write to Hans Wilhelm Traugott von Könneritz, Kapellmeister and Director of the Court Theatre in Dresden, to thank him for the fee of forty ducats he had received for a performance of *Fidelio* on 29 April in Dresden, conducted by Carl Maria von Weber. The name part had been taken by Wilhelmine Schröder-Devrient, who had sung in the Vienna revival at the end of 1822 and early 1823. In his letter Beethoven did not fail to take the opportunity to promote his *Missa Solemnis*, which he was hoping the King of Saxony would subscribe to.

On 13 August Beethoven abandoned the villa at Hetzendorf and moved to Baden, most likely for his health, but it may also have been because of Baron Müller, who was in the habit of greeting Beethoven with a deep bow whenever he saw him. Karl soon joined his uncle there, for when he left Blöchlinger's school at the end of the month it was for the last time. More letters to his family were occasioned by the illness of his brother Johann, and reports that had reached Ludwig that his sister-in-law, Johann's wife, had actually received her lover, and been seen in public with him, whilst her husband was confined to bed. Schindler now came in for a certain amount of abuse from Beethoven in his letters, despite his long-suffering attentions, and as soon as Karl joined him in Baden, he used him as his amanuensis.

It was while he was still at Baden that Carl Maria von Weber visited Beethoven, on 5 October, in atrocious weather, as he recorded both in his diary and in the letter he wrote subsequently to his wife. A member of the party on that occasion was Sir Julius Benedict, an English pupil of Weber's, who also set down his account of his time in Vienna, and was present at the first performance of the E flat quartet, Op. 127, on 6 March 1825, before he left. Benedict's account also helps us to fix the date of Beethoven's return to Vienna in the autumn of 1823, for he was back by 25 October, which was the date of the first performance of Weber's *Euryanthe* in Vienna.

Karl had left school when he was seventeen and was attending university in Vienna, so Beethoven felt that he could not in all conscience continue to accept half of his mother's pension towards the boy's education, so he wrote to Joseph Karl Bernard to this effect early in January 1824. He had heard that she was not well, and in straitened circumstances, and wanted to ensure that as long as he lived she should enjoy her full pension. Moreover, he wanted to make full provision for Karl in case he (Beethoven) should pre-decease her. He was also going to try to get Johann to contribute something as well, and he actually took over a debt of some 280 florins she owed to Steiner.

Not long after this, Beethoven received a letter from the *Gesellschaft der Musikfreunde* in Vienna, who had commissioned an oratorio from him and paid an advance in 1819. The fault was not entirely Beethoven's, for Bernard had not completed the libretto until the

end of October 1823, and the *Gesellschaft* had then waited for more than two months before taking action. In his reply, dated 23 January 1824, Beethoven made several points, some of which were valid and some of which were not. He said that he had not chosen Bernard to write the text, which was true. On the other hand, he said that the 400 florins had been sent to him without his having asked for them, and that he would have returned them long ago if he had realised what was going to happen. It is much to the *Gesellschaft's* credit that they did not take umbrage at this reply, and even made him an honorary member later on, despite the fact that they never received the oratorio or the return of the advance.

It would seem from the correspondence of this time – i.e. February and early March 1824 – that the ninth symphony was finished and was being copied. Beethoven had in fact told the Archduke Rudolph in a letter written on 1 July of the previous year, 1823, that he hoped that the symphony would be finished in less than a fortnight. People had by then doubtless learned to take Beethoven's estimates with a large pinch of salt. On 20 February 1824 Beethoven received a gold medal from Louis XVIII of France, which is now in the *Gesellschaft der Musikfreunde* in Vienna. In addition to agreeing to subscribe to the Mass, the king had also decided to honour Beethoven in this way. Then on 10 March Beethoven replied to Schott in Mainz, who had asked him to contribute to their publication *Cäcilia*, and had asked him whether he had any works for publication. There was nothing unusual in such requests, and by now Beethoven was quite used to them. However, it is worth drawing attention to this particular instance, because it was ultimately Schott who were to publish the *Missa Solemnis*, Op. 123; the ninth symphony, Op. 125; the first of the late string quartets, Op. 127, and then the C sharp minor quartet, Op. 131.

By now, however, Beethoven was involved in arrangements for the concerts of 7 May and 23 May that were to bring the ninth symphony and parts of the *Missa Solemnis* to the Viennese public, though the first complete performance of the latter took place in April 1824 in St Petersburg, organised by Prince Galitzin. Letters from Beethoven written to Count Dietrichstein in March show that the composer was trying to get the Grosser Redoutensaal for 8 April, since he could not have it for 7 April, though in the end the first concert was given on 7 May in the Kärntnerthor Theater, and

Liszt (1811-86) in his thirteenth year, from a lithograph by Leprince. It was when he was only eleven that Liszt is supposed to have been taken by Czerny to play for Beethoven in the Schwarzspanierhaus in Vienna, and received a kiss on the forehead from the composer as a token of the latter's esteem.

that of 23 May in the Grosser Redoutensaal. In addition to the ninth symphony and the overture *The Consecration of the House*, Op. 124, Beethoven gave three items from the *Missa* in the first concert, and only one – the Kyrie – in the second, together with the vocal trio *Tremate, empi, tremate*, Op. 116, and an aria by Rossini, *Di tanti palpiti*, transposed for tenor.

The concert was a very harrowing experience for Beethoven. At times he despaired of ever giving it, since he felt that the Viennese public would not understand the music of his ninth symphony and the *Missa*, being more interested in what he regarded as the superficial music of Rossini. He was also worried about the financial aspect, and from the conversation books for January that year it is evident that the singer Henriette Sontag was trying to give him sufficient moral courage to go ahead. If he agreed to put on the concert, then she would see to it that there was a full house. She told him that he lacked self-confidence, and that there would be no great opposition, simply people who wanted to hear his music. Even so, Beethoven was seriously contemplating having the works performed in Berlin, though when the news got around, thirty of his friends and admirers signed a document, beseeching him not to do so. Unfortunately this only proved to Beethoven that there was opposition, since the story then circulated that he had prompted the writing and publication of the petition himself. On reflection, however, he accepted it in the spirit in which it was intended, and agreed to give the concert.

There were seemingly endless discussions of detail, and as late as 21 April the concert was still officially to be held in the Theater an der Wien. Then there was censorship trouble, since liturgical texts were to be performed in a theatre, and when Beethoven's letter of explanation to the censor – in which he said that the works were to be designated 'hymns' on the programme – failed in its objective, the intervention of Count Lichnowsky had to be sought. Somehow the work was put on, with Beethoven officially conducting, but in fact Umlauf directed. Despite what must have been a good deal of strangeness in it to Viennese ears, the music pleased, and at the timpani solo in the scherzo of the symphony, the audience burst into applause. When the work was over, Beethoven was still turning over the pages of the score, and had to be turned round to acknowledge the applause of an enthusiastic audience.

From a musical point of view the concert was an undoubted success, but financially it fell far below Beethoven's expectations, and there was little more than the sum of 400 florins after the expenses had been paid. Tradition has it that when Beethoven received the news he fell down in a dead faint and had to be carried to his bed, where he was found by his servants the next morning, still in his clothes of the night before. Even if

The title page of the score of the string quartet,
Op. 131, as published by Schott. When Gerhard von
Breuning pointed out to Beethoven that the work had
not been well received when performed by
Schuppanzigh's quartet, the composer merely remarked:
'One of these days they will like it.'

this version is somewhat exaggerated, there is no doubt that he was bitterly disappointed, and all his old suspicions and fears about putting on the concert in Vienna in the first place were now confirmed. Shock soon turned to anger and spite, however, and he invited Schindler, Umlauf and Shuppanzigh to eat with him at the restaurant in the Prater known as *Zum wilden Mann*. Beethoven was accompanied by his nephew Karl, and it was not long before he accused the management and the hapless Schindler of having cheated him. It seems as if Beethoven's brother Johann had spurred him on to this accusation, and certainly Johann was jealous of Schindler's place in Beethoven's life. Schindler must have tried to defend himself, and yet the letter that Beethoven wrote to him shortly after the concert shows how Beethoven chose to reward faithful service. In it Beethoven told Schindler how he had always been worried that one day, sooner or later, some misfortune would fall him because of Schindler, and on the day that they had eaten together in the Prater, Beethoven

was convinced that Schindler had harmed him seriously. The composer found his very presence irritating, and bitterly resented the man's attempts to humour him when he seemed out of sorts. He found Schindler vulgar, and rash, and other people had simply confirmed Beethoven's opinion.

The second concert was even more of a disaster, for the weather was fine, and since it was billed for 12.30 in the middle of a Sunday, the house was less than half full. There was a loss of some 800 florins, though Duport had guaranteed Beethoven the sum of 500, which he accepted with some reluctance. From a letter that Beethoven wrote to Tobias Haslinger after the performance, apologising that he had not received complimentary tickets, it was evident that Duport had introduced the vocal trio and the Rossini aria as a concession to popular taste, and he had also described the trio as a new work, when in fact it was some ten years old. Haslinger had bought the work, but had not yet published it.

For the summer Beethoven had rented a property at Penzing from 1 May, and moved into it towards the end of the month, but unfortunately the house, as admirably as it suited in almost every respect as far as Beethoven was concerned, was close to a footbridge over a stream, and people would stop on the bridge and look through the windows of Beethoven's rooms, which so infuriated him that he moved after some six weeks and at the end of July went to Baden Gutenbrunn, where he remained until November. It was from there that he wrote to Johann Baptist Bach on 1 August, thanking him for having recommended the house – Schloss Gutenbrunn – to him, since he was being very well looked after, and referring to his will, since he felt that he was destined to die of a stroke as his grandfather had. He therefore wanted to make sure that while Karl remained his sole heir, his brother was to have the Erard piano given him in 1803.

We learn from other letters written at this time that the weather was not good, thus delaying the cure that he was engaged on. From one dated 28 August to the publisher Probst in Leipzig, it is clear that Beethoven had already disposed of the *Missa* to Schott, but that he was still holding out the possibility of the ninth symphony: meanwhile swearing him to the greatest secrecy, of course. Probst did not get the symphony, however, even if he had wanted it, which seems doubtful, and that work and the quartet Op. 127 also went to Schott, though they had to wait some time before they received the scores. Beethoven kept writing with excuses for his failure to deliver them. On 17 September he said that he would see to the copying of the works as soon as he returned to Vienna, and would send the quartet by the middle of October. In November the excuse was that he had to give lessons of two hours each day to Archduke Rudolph, but on 5 December the works would be de-

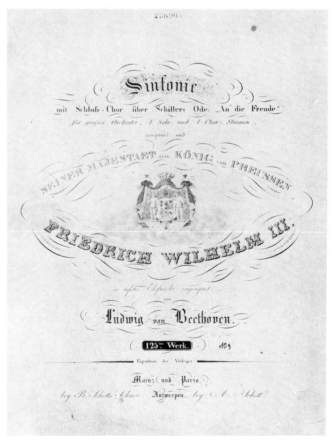

livered to Herren Fries and Co. that week. On 17 December it would be yet another week, and so the year went by without completion.

Meanwhile Peters must have heard that they were not to get the Mass or the quartet, and complained to Beethoven, who replied on 12 December that he had had to give the quartet as part of the deal with Schott in taking the Mass, but that Peters would get another quartet. Beethoven was in a difficult situation, from a moral point of view, since he had accepted money from Peters as an advance. However, he proposed to let them have another work, and the advance could then be deducted from this larger fee; in that way he might pay it back. At the same time he took them to task for having accused him of sending inferior works to them, whereas they themselves had asked for songs, marches and bagatelles. He accused them of having realised that they had offered too large a fee, and so now they were of the opinion that they could get something larger for it. Morally, however, it is difficult to exonerate Beethoven, since the fundamental point at issue was still the way in which he had tried to play off one publisher against the other.

A letter from Neate in London, dated 20 December 1824, informed Beethoven that the symphony had arrived there, and that the first rehearsal would take place on 17 January. In the letter Neate also issued an invitation on behalf of the Philharmonic Society for Beethoven to go to London. The idea obviously

The autograph dedication to Beethoven's ninth symphony, and the printed title page of the Schott score of 1826, with the arms and title of Friedrich Wilhelm III of Prussia.

*Henriette Sontag (1806-54). The celebrated singer
was only sixteen years old when she sang the soprano
part in the Ninth Symphony.*

appealed to him, though in the event came to nothing because they would not meet his demands, and even if they had done so it is still questionable whether he would have gone, for all his habitual doubts and fears, suspicions even, came to the fore, and undermined what resolution he might have.

There was some positive achievement at this time, however, for on 22 January 1825 Beethoven was able to write to Schott that he had, on 16 January, delivered the Mass and the symphony to Fries the banker, who would then forward them to the publishers. Then in February he agreed with Schuppanzigh on a date–6 March 1825–for the first performance of the Op. 127 quartet, the first of the three Galitzin quartets. Beethoven was so concerned about the first performance of this work that he got Schindler to draw up a document, which he then made the members of the quartet sign, promising that they would all do their best, and strive with each other in excellence. They duly did so, in pencil–Schuppanzigh, Weiss, Linke (who described himself as the great master's accursed cello), and Karl Holz (who was the last, 'but only in signing'). The appearance of Holz's name here is interesting, because he was to supplant Schindler as Beethoven's factotum until the composer's last illness, though we are forced to rely on Schindler for much of our information about the relationship between the composer and his new friend. The first performance of the quartet was not a success, so Beethoven gave it to Böhm's quartet, and it was their performance, on 23 March, that was the first truly successful one. Meanwhile, the ninth symphony had been given its first performance in London on 21 March, conducted by Smart for the Philharmonic Society.

Beethoven went to Baden on 7 May 1825. He was suffering from intestinal disorders at the time, and even allowing for a certain degree of hypochondria, was evidently not well. It was during this month, however, that he composed the third movement of the string quartet, Op. 132, which he described as a 'song of thanksgiving offered up to the Divinity by a convalescent'. In a letter to Karl dated 17-18 May, he wrote that he was beginning to compose again, though once more Karl himself was causing his uncle considerable concern. That spring he entered the Polytechnic Institute as a preparation for a career in business, and the deputy director of the institute was soon to become co-guardian in succession to Karl Peters. At the same time Karl went to live with the family of Matthias Schlemmer in Vienna, where he remained until the end of July the following year. A good deal of the correspondence that has survived from this summer is to Karl, and shows to what extent he had become involved in the composer's day-to-day existence and business dealings. There is also evidence of the growing importance of Holz, whose name in German means wood, and which therefore gave Beethoven several possibilities for the puns to which he was so much addicted. By 24 August, when writing to Karl, Beethoven referred to their 'piece of mahogany', and how energetic it was, and then expressed the belief that Holz would probably become one of their friends. In a letter of 3 September Beethoven told Holz to regard him as a *cantus firmus*, and indeed the next year Beethoven was to entrust the writing of his biography to Holz.

This letter is also of interest since it shows what progress the composer had made on the three Galitzin quartets. The first one, Op. 127, as we have already seen, had been finished by the end of February, been performed during March, and sent to Prince Galitzin that same month. The second, Op. 132, was finished by the end of July or the beginning of August, and the third, Op. 130, was being composed by this date, though it was not 'almost finished' as Beethoven wrote to the prince at the end of July. By the beginning of September arrangements were well in hand for a performance of the second quartet by Schuppanzigh. The Parisian publisher Moritz Schlesinger was anxious to hear it before he left Vienna, so he had a rehearsal in his rooms on 7 September. Others took place on 9 and 11, and performances were given on 6 and 20 November. Beethoven was anxious that nothing should go wrong, and indeed to some extent he was justified after the experience with the first Galitzin quartet. Nevertheless it says a great deal for his relationship with, and confidence in, Schuppanzigh, that he entrusted this new venture to him.

It so happened that Sir George Smart was in Vienna at this time, and his diary contains a most useful account of the rehearsal on 9 September:

Friday, September 9th.–We then went to Mecchetti's music shop . . . Mr. Holz, an amateur in some public office and a good violin player, came in and said Beethoven had come from Baden this morning and would be at his nephew's–Karl Beethoven, a young man aged twenty–No. 72 Alleegasse . . . At twelve I took Ries [a Viennese pianomaker, not the composer] to the hotel Wildemann [in fact the tavern *Zum wilden Mann*], the lodgings of Mr. Schlesinger, the music seller of Paris, as I understood from Mr. Holz that Beethoven would be there, and there I found him. He received me in the most flattering manner. There was a numerous assembly of professors to hear Beethoven's second new manuscript quartette, bought by Mr. Schlesinger. This quartette is three-quarters of an hour long. They played it twice. The four performers were Schuppanzigh, Holz, Weiss, and

The announcement of the first performance of the ninth symphony in Vienna, which took place in the Kärntnerthor Theater on 7 May 1824.

Lincke. It is most chromatic and there is a slow movement entitled 'Praise for the recovery of an invalid.' Beethoven intended to allude to himself I suppose for he was very ill during the early part of this year. He directed the performers, and took off his coat, the room being warm and crowded. A staccato passage not being expressed to the satisfaction of his eye, for alas, he could not hear, he seized Holz's violin and played the passage a quarter of a tone too flat. I looked over the score during the performance. All paid him the greatest attention.

Smart also attended the second full rehearsal on 11 September, and afterwards stayed to dinner, and then heard Beethoven extemporise on the piano. In all it was a happy evening, and the composer was in good spirits. Moreover, from Smart's account he was still able to hear some conversation. This was one aspect of the composer, but from the letters to his nephew, which continue throughout the summer and autumn, we see the other side of a character that seemed to be growing progressively more neurotic, possessive and hypochrondriac. On 4 October, for example, he expressed the hope that Karl would never have to feel ashamed of what the composer regarded as his nephew's callous behaviour towards him. Then with more insight he explained that when Karl saw him in a storming rage, it was because he was so anxious for the boy's well being and future. Then he returned to his illness again, reproaching Karl with all that he had to endure and which, in his opinion, ought not to be so. Then there was the fear lest he fall ill and be on his own. Indeed in a letter to Karl dated 12 October Beethoven even suggested that his nephew wanted him to die, and the tone of subsequent letters is positively hysterical.

On 15 October Beethoven returned to Vienna, to new lodgings in the Schwarzspanierhaus, which was to be his last address in the city. There he described himself, in a note to Karl Holz, like a shipwrecked mariner. However, things were to improve, for he was to find a housekeeper, Rosalie (Sali) who remained with him to the end, and he renewed an old friendship with the von Breunings, long fallen into decay, though without any actual rupture. It was as if through Stephan von Breuning's young son Gerhard, then aged thirteen, that a new light came to brighten the last months of the composer's life.

As an indication of Beethoven's international renown at this time, we may take as a fair example the account given in Sir John Russell's *A tour in Germany, and some of the southern provinces of the Austrian Empire, in 1820, 1821, 1822,* which was published in Edinburgh in 1828. Russell must therefore have been preparing his book for the press in the last months of the composer's life, for he added a footnote to the effect that Beethoven had died since he started writing, and that he died, moreover, in want, 'amid a people who pretend to be the most devoted worshippers of music and musicians'. Of Beethoven's status and image, however, the author – for one – was in no doubt:

> Beethoven is the most celebrated of the living composers in Vienna and, in certain departments, the foremost of his day. Though not an old man, he is lost to society in consequence of his extreme deafness, which has rendered him almost unsocial. The neglect of his person which he exhibits gives him a somewhat wild appearance. His features are strong and prominent; his eye is full of rude energy; his hair, which neither comb nor scissors seem to have visited for years, overshadows his broad brow in a quantity and confusion to which only the snakes round a Gorgon's head offer a parallel. His general behaviour does not ill accord with the unpromising exterior.

Russell goes on in this somewhat prissy vein, but concludes this description with what might either have been a totally fortuitous piece of imagery, or a profound understanding of Beethoven's true nature:

> The amateurs were enraptured; to the uninitiated it was more interesting to observe how the music of the man's soul passed over his countenance. He seems to feel the bold, commanding, and the impetuous, more than what is soothing or gentle. The muscles of the face swell, and its veins start out; the wild eye rolls doubly wild, the mouth quivers, and Beethoven looks like a wizard, overpowered by the demons whom he himself has called up.

There are plenty of people who would agree that there was something in Beethoven's nature that verged on the sinister, if not the evil, and his quarrels with, and mistrust of, those around him and most dedicated to his well-being is one of the saddest aspects of his behaviour.

Departure

THE ESTRANGEMENT between Stephan von Breuning and Beethoven had dated from the time that the former advised against the composer's becoming his nephew's guardian. There was no quarrel, but the friendship definitely waned from that time, and though they met occasionally, it seems to have been more by accident than design. In the Schwarzspanierhaus, however, Beethoven was a close neighbour of the von Breunings. During a visit to Vienna in August he met them in the street, and subsequently he received a good deal of hospitality from them whilst his new quarters were being got ready. On 20 September Beethoven wrote to Tobias Haslinger to ask how much a copy of Clementi's piano tutor would cost. He was only in Vienna from Baden for half a day, but he was evidently anxious to acquire a copy of the tutor for Gerhard von Breuning, whom he named *hosenknopf* (trouser button), or at other times, Ariel. Gerhard's mother seems to have overseen the organising of Beethoven's kitchen and the engaging of servants. This contact with the von Breunings in Vienna brought in its wake contact with Wegeler, whom he had not seen for twenty-eight years, and his wife Eleonore, Stephan's sister.

The beginning of 1826 found Beethoven in ill health again, with rheumatism or gout, as well as his old stomach complaint, and so Dr Braunhofer advised him to abstain from wine for a time, as well as coffee, whose stimulating effect was not good for Beethoven's condition. By March he would seem to have been a lot better, however. Unfortunately the correspondence is not particularly illuminating. We know that the third of the Galitzin quartets, Op. 130, was performed by Schuppanzigh and his friends on 21 March, however. They found the cavatina delightful, and indeed Holz maintained that the composer himself regarded it as the crowning achievement of his quartet writing. Simply to recall the music was sufficient to bring the tears to his eyes, and remember the tears of melancholy in which it was composed in the summer of 1825. Never before, so Holz maintained, had Beethoven's own music had such an effect on him. The fugue of the B-flat quartet caused problems for the players, as one might have expected, and it was Mathias Artaria's suggestion that the composer should write a new last movement, and that the original finale should be published separately, which it was, as Op. 133. The piano duet arrangement of the fugue by Beethoven was then published as Op. 134. A letter to Schott dated 20 May refers to the C sharp minor quartet, Op. 131, which he said was then finished, and on this occasion there seems no reason to doubt him. What is much less certain is that he had finished the last quartet in F, Op. 135, as would have been the case if a letter to Moritz Schlesinger dated 22 April is to be taken at face value. In that letter he said that the last quartet would be ready in two or three weeks at the latest. In fact it was only completed later in the year. Even so, it is obvious that the form of the quartet occupied Beethoven's creative mind almost exclusively at this period. There was still talk of an opera, and a letter of 31 May to Adolf Martin Schlesinger (Moritz's father) in Berlin, refers to Grillparzer's *Melusine* once more, and in theory Beethoven still was to write an oratorio.

In the summer of 1826, however, it was quite evident that a crisis was imminent with Karl, and it certainly exercised Beethoven's mind a great deal. It was increasingly clear that the guardianship was too much for the ailing composer, and in any case, in spite of all Beethoven's concern and exertions, Karl had been wasting his time drinking, playing billiards, frequenting dance halls and loose women – in short almost everything that the self-appointed father feared most. Then Beethoven considered the idea of taking his nephew into his apartment once again. Beethoven's brother

Johann acted as a kind of intermediary, and told the
composer that Karl could not bear the scenes that
always seemed to happen, both with himself and the
servants, and suggested that Ludwig ought to give up
the guardianship. That things were deteriorating
rapidly is beyond question. Holz arrived on one occasion to find that Karl had hold of his uncle by the front
of his coat, and by the end of July he had acquired a
pair of pistols.

After this, events moved rapidly. On Saturday 29
July Beethoven and Holz went to Schlemmer's house
where Karl lodged, and Schlemmer told the composer
that he had discovered a loaded pistol, with bullets and
powder, in a chest. He immediately cautioned Beethoven, and advised a sensitive approach to the boy, or
he would provoke him to desperate action. Schlemmer
said that Karl was in debt, but that this was only a part
of his current despair, and that there was also a cumula-
tive effect of guilty feelings from the past. At all events,
Schlemmer was convinced that Karl intended to take
his life. One can imagine the reaction this would provoke in Beethoven. Any intimation that Karl had a
mind of his own, as when he ran away, or saw his
mother without Beethoven's permission, was enough
to drive him to despair, but to learn that he actually
wanted to kill himself must have been shattering for
him.

Holz went immediately to the Polytechnic Institute
to fetch Karl, who said that he would return with him,
but wished first to collect some papers from a friend's
house. Holz – somewhat foolishly as it transpired –
waited for Karl at the institute and talked with Dr
Reisser, who learned of the existence of the gun with a
certain amount of cynical humour. When, after his
promised fifteen minutes, Karl did not come back to
the institute, Holz returned to Schlemmer's house and
told Beethoven what had happened. When the composer took Holz to task for letting Karl out of his sight,
he retorted that sooner or later the boy would have
given him – and the composer – the slip, and he had said
as much to Holz. Schlemmer then said that he had
found a second pistol. Beethoven was convinced that,
since Karl's guns had been discovered, he would drown
himself, but immediately they decided to go and see
Niemetz, a friend of Karl whom they hoped would
know of his intentions, and if they had no success, they
would then go to the police.

Karl, in the meantime, had gone to pawn his watch,
and with the money bought two more pistols, some balls
and powder. Judging it better not to return to his
lodging, he went out to Baden, where he spent the night

writing letters: one to his uncle, enclosed in a second to the friend Niemetz. The following morning, Sunday, he went up to the Rauhenstein ruins in the Helenthal so beloved by his uncle, and attempted to shoot himself. He was found by a passer-by, and taken to his mother's house in Vienna. When Beethoven arrived on the scene it was evident that he was the last person that he wanted to see. Holz then took a letter from Beethoven to Dr Smetana, the same doctor who had operated on Karl for his hernia, though in fact another doctor by the name of Dögl attended to him. Holz knew that there would have to be a police inquiry, and that in the circumstances Karl would probably receive a strong reprimand and then be kept under police observation afterwards. On 7 August Karl was removed from his mother's house by the police and taken to the general hospital, where he remained until 25 September. He had bungled the whole thing, though Holz maintained that if he had used the first set of pistols that Schlemmer discovered, then he most certainly would have killed himself, since they were loaded with a much heavier charge.

Karl always maintained that he grew worse because his uncle wanted him to be better, and as one looks back over the unhappy incident and the whole history of Beethoven's relationship with his nephew, one feels that the composer's concern was less for the boy's actual welfare and upbringing as a person, than out of commitment to some ideal concept that had no relation to the person of flesh and blood who stood before him. There was also not a little element of Beethoven's own pride at stake, and indeed when the news got around Vienna, despite the many expressions of sympathy, the once proud gait of the composer was completely bowed, and he bore himself, and looked, like a man of seventy.

The von Breunings, immediately after the event, invited Beethoven to take his meals with them so that he would not be on his own at such a critical time, and Stephan soon offered his advice on what was to be done when Karl was well enough to leave hospital. Though

A sketch for the cavatina of the string quartet,
Op. 130, which Beethoven regarded as the summit of
his writing in the medium, and his favourite movement.
He said that he composed it in tears of melancholy in
the summer of 1825.

Karl himself had previously mentioned a career in the army, Beethoven had never countenanced the idea. Now, however, since the trusted Stephan was a councillor in the war office, Beethoven was prepared to consider the idea more carefully. Throughout, Holz continued to be a tower of energy and strength, and all Beethoven's immediate friends united in trying to persuade him to give up the guardianship – which von Breuning then took up – and accept the idea of a military career for Karl. Brother Johann repeated his offer of a holiday at his house at Gneixendorf, which at first Beethoven refused in one of his shortest letters, dated 28 August: 'I will not come. Your brother ??????!!!! Ludwig.' In the event, however, Beethoven accepted his offer, for he was terrified as to what would become of Karl after he left hospital and before he joined the army. He did not want him to go to his mother's house, and at one stage even suggested that she should be sent away from Vienna so that there would be no risk of their meeting. So with considerable misgivings, since he could not entertain the thought of his sister-in-law without loathing, Beethoven and his nephew set out for Gneixendorf on 28 September, and arrived there the following day. The faithful Holz managed to find time to get married in the midst of all the arrangements for Beethoven's departure, which included getting a copy of the ninth symphony ready for despatch to the King of Prussia, to whom it was dedicated, and getting Haslinger to have it bound, as well as writing the letter to accompany it.

Gneixendorf did not offer the beautiful scenery of other places in which Beethoven had spent his summers away from Vienna, though he said that the view of the Danube reminded him of the Rhine. Whatever his misgivings or regrets, however, he must have been relieved that the immediate crisis had been resolved, whatever the cost to himself. The very name Gneixendorf, so he wrote to Haslinger, reminded him of a breaking axle, though he conceded that the air was healthy. Gradually he began to take up the threads of life once more, and wrote to Schott on 13 October with metronome markings for the ninth symphony, and also about the possibility of a collected edition of his works. So the days went by, and October passed on to November, and the two weeks that von Breuning had suggested for Karl's convalescence, and also for the scar caused by the bullet to be less obvious, had become two months. So on 1 December Beethoven and his nephew left Gneixendorf, and arrived in Vienna the next day. On the way the composer caught a chill, and had to take to his bed in the Schwarzspanierhaus. From his sickbed on 7 December he answered the letters written by Franz Gerhard Wegeler and his wife Eleonore from Coblenz almost a year previously, on 29 December 1825. At first Beethoven does not seem to have taken his illness very

Stephan von Breuning. His attempt to make Beethoven's life more regulated resulted in a quarrel, and it was only towards the end that their relationship was resumed on anything approaching its original warmth.

seriously, or thought that it was anything more than a temporary indisposition, though as time went by it became obvious that it was of a serious nature.

Karl acted as secretary initially, but preparations for joining the army began to involve him more and more. A bright moment was created by the arrival of forty volumes of Arnold's edition of the works of Handel, which Stumpff had promised in 1824. Gerhard von Breuning later recalled how he brought the books from the pianoforte to the bed for Beethoven, and what delight he took in looking through them. By this time dropsy had set in, however, and it was obvious that he would have to undergo an operation on 20 December to remove the water which had built up in his stomach.

Early in the New Year, on 2 January, Karl left Vienna to join his regiment at Iglau, and the next day Beethoven wrote to Johann Baptist Bach, naming Karl his sole heir. With the departure of Karl, Schindler now made his return as secretary. On 8 January Beethoven had to have a second operation, and on 3 February a third. Five days later he wrote to Stumpff to thank him for the gift of the Handel volumes, and then on 17 February he wrote to Wegeler again. In this letter he expressed the belief that a fourth operation was going to be necessary, which was true, since it took place ten days later. His spirits had been helped by the decision of Dr von Malfatti to forget past hurts, and come and give his professional aid, in addition to Dr Wawruch who was treating Beethoven. Von Malfatti suggested administering frozen punch, which at first had a beneficial effect, but then Beethoven seems to have imbibed too much of it, which only served to make his condition worse. Of course von Malfatti may well have felt that the case was hopeless, and that it was simply a matter of making the composer's end as comfortable as possible.

Wegeler and von Malfatti were not the only old friends who reappeared in these, the last stages of the composer's life. Nikolaus Zmeskall, himself a sufferer from gout, sent a message of sympathy, and in his reply Beethoven said that the worst thing was not being able to do anything. Even in this, his last illness, that amazing source of energy was bursting to be let out. Doubtless through Stumpff's intervention, the Philharmonic Society agreed to lend to its members, to send to Beethoven, the sum of £100 'to be applied to his comforts and necessities during his illness'. Baron Johann Pasqualati sent gifts of food and wine, and the Hummels

Johann Nepomuk Hummel (1778-1837), composer and piano virtuoso and to some extent Beethoven's rival. But his friend, also, who hastened to be with him in his last illness.

came to Vienna from Weimar as soon as they heard of his illness, and remained there until after his death. There was a rallying on 17 March, when Beethoven wrote to Schindler: 'Truly a miracle, miracle, miracle . . .' and praising von Malfatti's skill. On 23 March he made his last codicil to his will. That same day the Hummels, with the fifteen-year-old Ferdinand Hiller, paid their last visit to Beethoven. Three days later, according to Hiller, they were in the house of a former pupil of Hummel's, von Liebenberg, when a severe storm broke between five and six o'clock. There was a thick flurry of snow, loud thunder and flashes of lightning. When some guests arrived later they told them that Beethoven was dead, having passed away at 4.45 p.m. The date was 26 March 1827.

The death struggle, as befitted that Titan, lasted two days. Anselm Hüttenbrenner, amateur composer and friend of Schubert and Beethoven, and according to him the detested sister-in-law, Johann's wife, were the only witnesses of his death, though von Breuning, Schindler and the artist Johann Teltscher, brother Johann, Sali the housekeeper, and possibly a nurse, were all in and out of the room during the last hours. The dropsy was a symptom of the disease which finally carried him off, namely cirrhosis of the liver, though to that modern opinion has added the possibility that Beethoven also had syphilis.

The composer's funeral took place in the afternoon of 29 March at 3 p.m., and was one of the most impressive ever seen in Vienna. It was estimated that some 20,000 people crowded into the square in front of the Schwarzspanierhaus. The coffin was set in the courtyard, and a choir sang one of the *Equali* for trombones that Beethoven had composed at Linz in 1812, arranged by Seyfried to the words of the *Miserere*, and another to *Amplius lava me*. The pall bearers were eight *kapellmeisters*, including Hummel and Seyfried, and among the torch bearers were Schubert, Böhm, Czerny, Schuppanzigh, Holz, Linke and Grillparzer, who also wrote the funeral oration, which was delivered by the actor Anschütz at the gate of the cemetery at Währing, since the regulations did not permit public speaking within the cemetery precincts. The grave fell into disrepair, and on 13 October 1863 the *Gesellschaft der Musikfreunde* had the body exhumed and reburied, but it was not until 21 June 1888 that the remains were removed and taken to the central cemetery in Vienna, together with those of Schubert, who died in 1828, and the remains of the two men were placed side by side.

Vienna had realised all too late what Beethoven's real condition was. When the money from the Philharmonic Society arrived in Vienna, for example, the man charged with handing it over, Rau of the banking house of Eskeles, was genuinely amazed and distressed to discover that what was common knowledge in the musical circles of London was not even suspected by all but a tiny few in Vienna. In view of the state of the composer's health by then, however, there was little that could have been done for him, other than ensuring that his last days were as comfortable as possible. Although Beethoven had expressed a desire, in one of his last letters, that he might still be able to write some great works, one feels that after the last quartets, there was nothing left to say.

And yet, if this be so, where do we place Beethoven, for manifestly his music continues to speak to us as strongly today as it did then, and composers have continued to write music, some of which would be stranger to Beethoven's contemporaries by far than his music was to them. There is a tendency to think of Beethoven as the first of the great Romantic composers, but this needs careful consideration, and a closer examination of the historical perspective shows that this is not so. As we saw at the outset, Beethoven's family background and early career were well within the traditional framework for church and court musicians, and the fact that he himself continued, until quite late in his career, to contemplate and even hanker after a court appointment, shows to what extent he was a child of the old system.

A biographical notice, published in the Monthly Supplement to the Musical Library in London in 1834 shows us how he was thought of in the decade immediately after his death:

> Ludwig van Beethoven was born on the 17th of December, 1770, at Bonn, where his father and grandfather were both principal singers in the Elector's chapel. His father, who was too much devoted to the rites of Bacchus, neglected his education, and the first instructions he received in music were from Neefe, organist to the court. He afterwards went to Vienna, and studied composition for a short time under Haydn; but this great master was born to compose, not teach, and he discreetly made over his pupil to Albrechtsberger, who was born to teach, not to compose. He then returned to Bonn, though he soon obtained the Elector's permission again to visit Vienna, where he finally settled, and we believe never quitted that city and its environs during the remainder of his life. He was once strongly solicited by Jérôme Bonaparte to become *Maestro di Capella* to the new court of Westphalia, but the archduke Rudolph, influenced more by shame than any better feeling, settled on him an annuity, on condition of his not quitting the Austrian dominions without permission. The Philharmonic Society of London offered him an invitation to this capital, and

Lyser's sketch of Beethoven. It was said that after the attempted suicide of his nephew Karl, Beethoven walked, and looked, like a man of seventy.

he was on the point of accepting it, but his increased deafness, which had rendered it impossible to converse with him, except in writing, prevented his undertaking so distant a journey. His works are exceedingly numerous, but no record is left to tell us when and for what purpose composed.

There are some errors of fact which the reader will be aware of, as for example the placing of the lessons with Haydn in the first visit to Vienna rather than the second, and the total omission of any reference to Mozart. However, the most interesting feature of this passage, in the present context, is the last sentence. Here again, the account is not quite accurate, for many of the early works were composed for special occasions or for court

Einladung

zu

Ludwig van Beethoven's

Leichenbegängniss,

welches am 29. März um 3 Uhr Nachmittags Statt finden wird.

Man versammelt sich in der Wohnung des Verstorbenen im Schwarzspanier=Hause Nr. 200, am Glacis vor dem Schottenthore.

Der Zug begibt sich von da nach der Dreyfaltigkeits=Kirche bey den P. P. Minoriten in der Alsergasse.

Die musikalische Welt erlitt den unersetzlichen Verlust des berühmten Tondichters am 26. März 1827 Abends gegen 6 Uhr. Beethoven starb an den Folgen der Wassersucht, im 56. Jahre seines Alters, nach empfangenen heil. Sacramenten.

Der Tag der Exequien wird nachträglich bekannt gemacht von

L. van Beethoven's
Verehrern und Freunden.

(Diese Karte wird in Tob. Haslingers Musikhandlung vertheilt.)   Gedruckt bey Anton Strauß.

An invitation to Beethoven's funeral on 29 March 1827, and a watercolour of the procession, which was attended by some 20,000 people, by F. Stöber.

celebrations, and even later in Beethoven's career, *The Battle of Vittoria*, for example, was composed for a special purpose. Even so, for most of Beethoven's music there could be no question of its needing to have a purpose. It was composed because Beethoven had to communicate what was in his mind. Of course he wrote to commission, and he responded to circumstances, but the great masterpieces were his alone. Nor was their formulation in any way easy, let alone facile, for composition did not come especially easily to him.

When Haydn and Beethoven sent a group of compositions to the elector back in Bonn–as it were an offering of the first fruits of the pupil's labours–and the elector retorted that if this was all he had to show for his expensive time in Vienna then he might as well go back to Bonn, he may seem somewhat boorish to us today, but in the context of his own day he was displaying a perfectly normal reaction, namely that music was composed for a purpose, that it was in fact akin to an artisan's craft that was transmitted through learning, and was offered for consumption rather as a consumer commodity. Beethoven's example was to change all that. After him, the composer would be able to exist independently, both financially and artistically, and in this he certainly opened the door for posterity, and stood on the threshold of Romanticism, even though he himself remained in the domain of Classicism.

Of course Beethoven was not the first to do this. Mozart had tried, but had, in purely material terms, failed. Beethoven had difficulty, also, though we know that he often made out to be poorer than he really was, especially later in his career. Or we can go farther back, to Handel, who despite his court salaries nevertheless operated on his own account in the opera world. The difference was that Handel was giving the public what they wanted, and if they indicated that they no longer wanted opera, then he turned to oratorio. It is only fair to Handel to say that he did a great deal to educate the public taste in this matter, and that in oratorio he was able to give expression to some of his most sublime music. However, even his strongest champions could not maintain that he was an innovator in any way comparable to Beethoven. This is by no means to suggest that it is only the innovators who are truly great, whether it be in music or any of the creative arts, and indeed one of the most unfortunate phenomena of the post-Romantic era has been the restless search for new forms, new modes of expression, especially in the twentieth century. There has also been the concomitant tendency to evaluate composers, to place them in a kind of league table of their relative degrees of greatness, as if this made the slightest difference to their music or our response to it.

Throughout the history of art there have been the innovators, and those who went on their way honestly pursuing their craft. As the great conductor Koussevitsky has said:

> Every great, or less great, or even little, composer brings something to the art of music which makes the art great in its entirety. Each one brings his portion. In examination of his music we can see how real a composer is. We can see whether his technique is perfect; whether he knows how the orchestra and the individual instruments sound and whether or not he has something to say, no matter what the degree of importance. Sometimes a single man has one single word to say in all his life and that one word may be as important as the lifework of a great genius. We need that word –and so does the genius himself need that word.

It is perhaps ironical that Beethoven, who is widely regarded as the 'greatest' composer the world has ever known, should have set the pattern for this concept of greatness in the Romantic tradition, whereas the whole of his life was devoted to establishing the right of the composer to say his 'word' in the Koussevitsky sense. We seem now, however, to have gone as far as it is possible to go down that particular path, and have almost reached the point where individuality and abstruseness seem to be the only criteria for evaluating new works, which is a most unfortunate state of affairs. If it is easy to listen to, too easy to listen to, then it cannot be good. If it is difficult, and probably unlovely, then it is probably good.

Of course there is a problem of musical language which exists today, and has existed ever since the disintegration of tonality on a large scale. In Beethoven's day he was able to use the music of his time as a springboard, and had he been able to hear more of the contemporary music of his day as he grew older, he may have written differently. From this point of view his deafness forced his musical culture to be arrested in its development. Even so, there was a common musical language, whereas today there is a schism, whereby a composer is faced with the prospect of writing in what is still a largely esoteric tongue for the majority of music lovers, or capitulating to what, by contemporary standards, is a dead tradition. In time the ear of the public at large may well be educated to accepting and understanding the idiom of contemporary music, but at present chaos reigns. There are some contemporary 'classics', and some of our most gifted musical talents are today devoted to propagating them. Unfortunately there is also a great deal of bigotry, and those who cannot readily accept contemporary music are accused of being out of date. Time alone will show who is right, but what is most regrettable is that an artistic élite has been created, and 'contemporary' music, that was once

Franz Schubert, seen here in a sketch by W. A. Rieder, who died only a year after Beethoven, in 1828.

the heritage of all, has now become the preserve of a select few.

The problem is enormous, and one simplifies it at one's peril. The great French musical pedagogue Nadia Boulanger has expressed it in this way:

> If we put from us the works of the Past, and deny ourselves the emotions they diffuse, we are in fact denying the possibility of survival to contemporary art.
>
> If we diminish their power, we diminish that of art in general, for nothing could be reborn from the destruction. But to stop dead, so as only to contemplate what has been, is just as great a mistake.
>
> Now, two opposite phenomena occur: either an exaggerated tendency to look upon our own epoch as decadent; or a propensity–

no less exaggerated–to consider as worthwhile only that which is being produced at the present time. The infinite variety in life dominates these anxieties, and gives each event more real greatness and less exterior importance. That which is sincere, that which is beautiful, does not become petrified.

Here, then, is a statement of the problem, and a very rational solution to it, though admittedly written more than fifty years ago, before the great divide that has taken place in music with the advent of dodecaphonic composition, and all that has followed. It would be very difficult for Nadia Boulanger to state that belief with quite the same degree of confidence today. In the wake of her adored Stravinsky she was more or less compelled to re-examine her attitude to modern music, and take more account of it. But her basic conclusion must surely stand, and ought to be repeated often. If she is felt to be too partisan on the side of 'classical' music, then this is what W. H. Auden had to say about the creative process in general:

Behind the work of any creative artist there are three principal wishes: the wish to make something; the wish to perceive something, either in the external world of sense or the internal world of feeling; and the wish to communicate these perceptions to others. Those who have no interest in or talent for making something, i.e. no skill in a particular artistic medium, do not become artists; they dine out, they gossip at street corners, they hold forth in cafés. Those who have no interest in communication do not become artists either; they become mystics or madmen.

There were plenty of people who thought that Beethoven was mad, or simply perverse on occasions, but no one could deny that his chief aim was to communicate, and in this he well illustrates Auden's description of the motivation of the creative artist. Indeed, one might almost say that without Beethoven the above could scarcely have been written, for he was the creative artist *par excellence*, and certainly the first 'subjective' composer. We know him as we know few other composers that went before him. Previously one tends to have the music and the man, in various proportions, but Beethoven was the first–apart from Mozart–to make it virtually impossible to divorce the music from the man.

This was, to a large degree, recognised in his own day. To revert to the biographical notice already quoted from 1834, the author went on:

> His temper deterred his friends from much intercourse with him, and his infirmity no doubt contributed much to his apparently unsociable disposition. His greatest works–and in these who has excelled him?–are his symphonies and overtures. When it seemed that his two great predecessors, Haydn and Mozart, had exhausted all the materials that fancy and art were able to supply, his imagination 'created new', and in devoting his powers to the same kind of composition in which his illustrious countrymen had shone with so much brilliancy, he never made himself their debtor for a single thought. He immediately followed them too in quartets, quintets, and sonatas, songs, cantatas, etc., but without ever borrowing from them, intentionally or by accident, an idea. Beethoven died of dropsy at Vienna, on the 26th of March, 1827, and received more honours at his funeral than ever were bestowed on him while living!

This almost complacent account of his life and work ought not, however, be allowed to blind us to the fact that Beethoven became known, and indeed did little or

Wagner (1813-83), who took to new limits some of the tendencies announced in, or foreshadowed by, Beethoven's life and work as a composer in the grand manner.

nothing to prevent himself from becoming known, to the world at large. This is why he is such a modern character. We see and recognise in him so much of our own experience, whether we have aspirations as creators or not, in coming to terms with society, and indeed the world at large. Whereas previous generations have tended to play down the less laudable aspects of his character, today we feel that they serve to enhance his humanity. To a certain extent this is perfectly fair and reasonable, since after the example of Beethoven the full-blown heroes of the Romantic era tended to think of themselves, and project themselves consciously, as characters that were larger than life, standing out above the common herd. Many of them consciously cultivated the mystique of the creative artist and the role of inspiration, or at best did little to dispel it, in a way that would have seemed almost incomprehensible to Beethoven, and towards the end the egocentricity, and assumption of the trappings of a genius, tended to increase as the amount of originality diminished. Nowadays we have several composers who have utterly rejected such concepts, and seek only to be at the service of society. A century and a half after his death, and

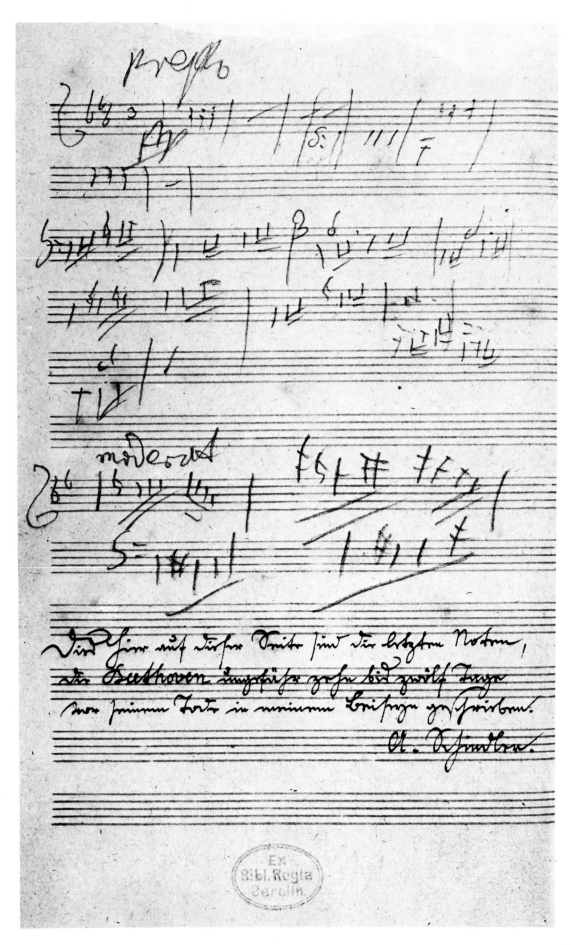

Some of the last music Beethoven wrote: sketches for
the tenth symphony, with annotation by A. Schindler.

some two centuries after his birth, the process set in train by Beethoven has run its course, and the wheel has turned full circle.

Perhaps not exactly full circle, however, for one can never put the clock back, however much one would like to. Because of Beethoven, things would never be the same as far as composers, and indeed music in general, were concerned. Moreover without his example the world would have been denied some of its finest music. But whereas today the composer is obliged to consider himself in relation to society, and undergo what is often a very hard struggle to communicate, to find his niche, for Beethoven there was no problem, certainly not in that realm. Music was an essential part of day-to-day life. People listened to it avidly, and were always hungry for more. This had the unfortunate effect of encouraging many composers to write too much music, or sacrifice quality to quantity, and much perfunctory or superficial music was written. Some composers simply could not keep pace, and with so much music being written and performed, a great deal was rapidly consigned to oblivion without much thought given to its intrinsic value. One cannot blame them for this, it was a fundamental aspect of the role of music and musicians in society. It is no accident that Bach was known in his own day chiefly as an organist, and that the works we prize so highly now were written within, and almost in addition to, his official functions.

Beethoven, too, began to make his name primarily as a virtuoso, and then subsequently as a composer, and in this he was helped by the traditions of musical life in Vienna as he found them. But all that was to change. For one thing, society was changing, and the role of music in society. Beethoven was the bridge between the old and the new. He started off his career in the service of a temporal ruler, as musicians had done for centuries before him, but after Beethoven, no ruler was ever again able to look upon a composer as his servant. Even if one cites the example of Wagner and Ludwig of Bavaria, it is at once very evident which foot the boot was on. Beethoven might well use the old forms of aristocratic patronage and dedications so as to get his music performed and published, and the music might well remain the technical property of those individuals for a given period of time, but once that music was written, it belonged only to the world at large, and even – as Beethoven himself said on one occasion – to future generations.

Beethoven was able to take advantage of the fact that there was little consciousness on the part of the concert-going public of any division between old and new music, Classical or Romantic, let alone traditional and avant-garde. They simply loved music, were used to hearing it, and therefore approached everything with a relatively open mind. Never again, in the history of music, was a composer to have such favourable conditions – patronage without constraint (despite what he may have felt or said about Archduke Rudolph, for example), and an educated musical public with little or no prejudice. Of course this is an extreme simplification. Beethoven spent much of his time and energy lamenting the fact that he had to work for money, and there were obviously those for whom his music was incomprehensible. Nevertheless he was appreciated during his lifetime, and acknowledged as a genius.

Herein lies the enigma, the tension, between the genius and the all too human being. After Beethoven we learned to expect our geniuses to be larger than life, great Romantic figures not quite of this world, with characters to match. Eccentricity fitted well into this scheme of things, and a turbulent love life was probably quite acceptable, too, as long as it was not too scandalous. As long as everything was on the grand scale, that was all that mattered. It comes as a somewhat un-

Beethoven in life. A copy of the life mask which was taken by Franz Klein in 1812 for the famous bronze bust. By this time the composer's deafness was well advanced, and there is great poignancy in the determination clearly shown in his powerful features.

pleasant duty, therefore, to have to admit that apart from the music, there is little in Beethoven's character that was particularly noble or inspiring. True, he did suffer a great disability, and true he was capable of purely charitable gestures – though even these were at times seen as a step in forwarding his own ends – but against all this one must set what by any standards are not the attributes of the spirit of genius.

From what we have learned of Beethoven's childhood, a great deal may be readily explained by his earliest environment and upbringing. The contrast between father and mother, the feeling of emotional and financial insecurity; this explains much. Then later in life the acute sensitivity to his deafness, his increasing ill health generally; these also explain a great deal. What is much harder to make excuses for is his lack of charity towards other human beings. He was, after all, a professed lover of mankind, and it is the humanity of his music that is the key to its greatness. How, then, does one explain away the suspicion, the ingratitude, the intrigue and downright unpleasantness so often evident in his dealings with his long-suffering friends? We all treat our friends badly from time to time, indeed to a certain extent it is part of the office of a friend to be treated badly, but Beethoven seems to have had little conception of what genuine loyalty and devotion were.

As far as servants were concerned, the indictment is even more serious. At times he was positively malevolent, and cruel to a degree inadmissible in a person professing to have any love of humanity. The idea that he would take into his employ a hunchback so that he would then be able to use his disability as a weapon against him is distinctly nasty. He was always ready to believe the worst of his servants – or of anyone, if it came to that – and he did not seem to have the faintest idea how to handle them.

These tendencies showed no abatement with the advance of years, when one might have expected a more benign face. On the contrary, they persisted and, if anything, increased in severity. The same is true of his dubious dealings with publishers. There was a time when, in order to protect himself and obtain the best conditions, a certain amount of chicanery was understandable, but there came a point when, as he himself said, there were several firms ready to publish whatever he offered them, and he was virtually in a position to name his own price. It was as if, having indulged in this sort of behaviour for so long, it almost became second nature to him, and he could not rid himself of it. In this, as in his dealings with friends and servants, he seemed to have no idea that trust would breed trust, and that the converse was equally true.

When it comes to a consideration of his dealings with his nephew Karl, then it would seem reasonably certain that there was definitely some psychological imbalance,

though exacerbated by Beethoven's own personality, of course. It may well be that all the pent-up emotions of years of thwarted love for women that never led on to matrimony, coupled with the lack of any filial affection of his own, made him latch on to Karl so possessively, and with such obsession, but it is more than likely that the tragedy would never have happened if he had been able to leave the boy to grow up naturally. It was as if, not having a son of his own, Beethoven was determined to give to the world something of himself that would survive him. As if his music was not sufficient. In such a situation one cannot blame the person, the chosen one, if he is unable to live up to the demands of a role he never wanted and is in any case ill-equipped to play. Unfortunately Beethoven was apparently unable to realise this, and even if he did, then his pride would not allow him to acknowledge the fact.

Schindler maintained that Beethoven told him that it was his sincere desire that whatever was said of him subsequently would adhere strictly to the truth in every respect, regardless of who might be hurt thereby, himself not excepted. Was that intended to be taken literally? We must assume so, and yet in Beethoven's case it has been the cause of much heartsearching on the part of those anxious to determine the truth. It certainly filled Thayer with dismay the farther he progressed with his monumental biography, to the point where he became reluctant to pursue it. Hopefully the fashion for debunking biographies has now passed away, and there can be few people, if any, who would take pleasure in retailing unpleasantness for its own sake. In the case of Beethoven one attempts to be dispassionate, avoiding romanticising the unattractive, and giving due acknowledgment to the good.

In the present climate there is a tendency to excuse the unattractive by weighing against it the music; that Beethoven had the courage to live out his life, and produced such remarkable music in so doing, then we can forgive him the rest. In terms of his gift to mankind, not only in his music, but in demonstrating what the individual can achieve in the face of all odds, then possibly we ought to go along with this view. The correlation between a man's life and his work is a constant problem. In some cases it is of no importance, or so it would seem, whereas in others the connection is a strong one, and is instructive in one's understanding of the work.

In the case of Beethoven it is true to say that he produced some of his most beautiful music in the face of enormous difficulties, and this certainly gives him nobility, since it elevates to a higher plane man's struggle with his condition, and his ability to overcome it. In this Beethoven is, along with Hamlet, a truly universal figure. We may all identify with him on this level, and as we are all Hamlets when we watch the play, so we are all Beethovens when we consider his life and work.

There are only two aspects which continue to nag at this concept. The first is that Beethoven never changed, never improved as the years went by, and success and the manifest devotion, even affection, of friends seemed unable to help him. The second is the lurking suspicion that at times he deliberately provoked unpleasantness, almost as if it were a drug that was necessary before he could create, or a sacrifice required as a necessary prelude to conception. If the reply to this is simply that he was first and foremost a human being, and that one cannot have the good without the bad, since that is what the majority of human nature is like, then there is no more to say. It is not Beethoven's fault if he set in train the Romantic concept of the noble genius, and then finds himself condemned by it.

Of course attitudes change, and almost every age must look at the composer anew, and as views on man and society change, so opinions on Beethoven change. Even so, he did express certain things that will be true for mankind, no matter how much tastes and fashions vary. There was no humbug about Beethoven. Whatever he did, he did with conviction and commitment, however unpleasant that might have been at times. He may well have been blinded by prejudice on occasion, or deeply misguided, as in his treatment of his nephew, but he did so entirely in good faith. He was, in his own terms, a realist. He lied with deliberate intent, there was never any attempt to explain it away, or salve his religious conscience. He knew right and wrong, and if, for some reason or other, he chose wrong, then he did so in full realisation. In an era when our permissiveness has blurred the dividing line between good and bad, this aspect is easily overlooked. It was one that was apparent to E. M. Forster almost seventy years ago, when he wrote *Howards End*, and what was true then, is no less true today:

> The goblins really had been there. They might return–and they did. It was as if the splendour of life might boil over and waste to steam and froth. In its dissolution one heard the terrible, ominous note, and a goblin, with increased malignity, walked quietly over the universe from end to end. Panic and emptiness! Panic and emptiness! Even the flaming ramparts of the world might fall.

> Beethoven chose to make all right in the end. He built the ramparts up. He blew with his mouth for the second time, and again the goblins were scattered. He brought back the gusts of splendour, the heroism, the youth, the magnificence of life and of death, and, amidst vast roarings of a superhuman joy, he led his Fifth Symphony to its conclusion. But the goblins were there. They could return. He had said so bravely, and that is why one can trust Beethoven when he says other things.

That is one truth that Beethoven proclaimed, and which will remain a truth no matter what man's attitude to morality becomes. The second is his vision of the good. It was as if, having made the reality of evil a matter beyond discussion, he then went on to give man a vision of all that is good and beautiful, too. The *heiliger Dankgesang* of the A minor quartet, Op. 132, was brilliantly described by Aldous Huxley in the last chapter of *Point Counter Point* in this way:

> Slowly, slowly, the melody unfolded itself. The archaic Lydian harmonies hung on the air. It was an unimpassioned music, transparent, pure and crystalline, like a tropical sea, an Alpine lake. Water on water, calm sliding over calm; the according of level horizons and waveless expanses, a counterpoint of serenities. And everything clear and bright; no mists, no vague twilights. It was the calm of still and rapturous contemplation, not of drowsiness or sleep. It was the serenity of the convalescent who wakes from fever and finds himself born again into a realm of beauty. But the fever was 'the fever called living' and the rebirth was not into this world; the beauty was unearthly, the convalescent serenity was the peace of God. The interweaving of Lydian melodies was heaven.

We may not accept the idea of God, or even that of heaven, but in a world that is becoming increasingly dehumanised, we very much need this vision of peace offered by Beethoven. So there are the two extremes of human experience–the worldly, and the other worldly– and between there is the distillation of pure joy that is the common experience of mankind.

Catalogue of Works

Opus numbers, where given, are those under which the works were originally published. WoO. stands for *Werke ohne Opuszahl* (Works without opus numbers), according to the Kinsky-Halm catalogue of 1955 (*see* Select Bibliography). Where no such data are provided, none is currently available.

Operas
Vestas Feuer (1803), incomplete. Libretto by Schikaneder.
Fidelio, Op. 72 (1804-05), in version known as *Leonore*; 1806, and 1814). The original libretto by Sonnleithner, based on Bouilly's *Léonore, ou l'amour conjugal*, was revised first by von Breuning, and then by Treitschke, and the original three acts were reduced to two.

Ballets
Ritterballet, WoO. 1 (1790-91).
The Creatures of Prometheus, Op. 43 (1800-01).

Incidental music
Two arias for *Die schöne Schusterin*, by Umlauf, WoO. 91 (1796).
Egmont, Op. 84 (1810), to a play by Goethe.
The Ruins of Athens, Op. 113 (1811), to a play by Kotzebue.
King Stephan, Op. 117 (1811), to a play by Kotzebue.
Triumphal march and introduction to Act II for *Tarpeja*, WoO. 2 (1813), to a play by Kuffner.
Germania, WoO. 94 (1814), final chorus for *Die gute Nachricht*, by Treitschke.
Leonora Prohaska, WoO. 96 (1815), to a play by Duncker.
Es ist vollbracht, WoO. 97 (1815), final chorus to *Die Ehrenpforten*, by Treitschke.
March with chorus, Op. 114 (1811), arranged from *The Ruins for Athens* for;
The Consecration of the House, Op. 124 (1822), overture in C for the opening of the Josephstadt Theater, Vienna, and including chorus with soprano solo, WoO. 98, to words by Meisl.

Sacred choral music with orchestra
The Mount of Olives, Op. 85 (1803, revised 1804), oratorio to words by Huber.

Mass in C, Op. 86 (1807).
Missa Solemnis in D, Op. 123 (1819-23).

Secular choral music with orchestra
Cantata on the death of Joseph II, WoO. 87 (1790), words by Averdonk.
Cantata on the accession of Leopold II, WoO. 88 (1790), words by Averdonk.
Fantasia for piano, chorus and orchestra, Op. 80 (1808), words by Kuffner.
Der glorreiche Augenblick, Op. 136 (1814), cantata to words by Weissenbach.
Chor auf die verbündeten Fürsten, WoO. 95 (1815), words by Bernard.
Meeresstille und glückliche Fahrt, Op. 112 (1815), words by Goethe.
Opferlied (1822), first choral setting of words by Matthisson.
Bundeslied, Op. 122 (1822-23), words by Goethe.
Opferlied, Op. 121b (1824), second choral setting of words by Matthisson.
Choral Symphony, Op. 125–last movement.
(*See* **Symphonies**.)

Secular choral music with piano
Trinklied, WoO. 109 (*c.* 1787).
Kriegslied der Österreicher, WoO. 122 (1797), words by Friedelberg.
Punschlied, WoO. 111 (*c.* 1790).
Der freie Mann, WoO. 117 (1791-92), words by Pfeffel.
O care selve, WoO. 119 (1795), words by Metastasio.
Un lieto brindisi, WoO. 103 (1814), words by Bondi.
Hochzeitlied, WoO. 105 (1819), words by Stein.
Cantata for Prince Lobkowitz's birthday, WoO. 106 (1823).

Vocal ensemble with orchestra
Nei giorni tuoi felici, WoO. 93 (1802-03), duet to words by Metastasio.
Tremate, empi, tremate, Op. 116 (1814), trio to words by Bettoni.
Sanft wie du lebtest, Op. 118 (1814), quartet.

Vocal ensemble with piano

Merkenstein, Op. 100 (1814-15), duet to words by Rupprecht. Also set as a solo song, WoO. 144 (1814).

Vocal ensemble unaccompanied

26 Italian duets, trios and quartets, WoO. 99 (1792-*c.* 1802), to words by Metastasio.

Lob auf den Dicken, WoO. 100 (1801), to words by the composer.

Graf, Graf, liebster Graf, WoO. 101 (1802), to words by the composer.

Abschiedsgesang, WoO. 102 (1814), to words by Seyfried.

Gesang der Mönche, WoO. 104 (1817), to words by Schiller.

48 canons for 3 to 6 voices, WoO. 159-198 and 203 (1795-1826), to words by various authors.

10 musical quips and word settings, WoO. 205 (*c.* 1798-1826).

Ich bin der Herr von zu (written in the sketchbook for *Der glorreiche Augenblick*, Op. 136), WoO. 199 (*c.* 1814?).

Holz, Holz, WoO. 204 (1825), canon on Holz's name.

Solo songs with orchestra

Prüfung des Küssens, WoO. 89 (*c.* 1790).

Mit Mädeln sich vertragen, WoO. 90 (*c.* 1790), to words by Goethe.

Ah perfido!, Op. 65 (1796), to words by Metastasio.

Primo amore, WoO. 92 (*c.* 1800).

No, non turbati, WoO. 92a (1801-02), to words by Metastasio.

Solo songs with piano

Schilderung eines Mädchens, WoO. 107 (1783).

An einen Säugling, WoO. 108 (1783), to words by Döhring.

Elegie auf den Tod eines Pudels, WoO. 110 (*c.* 1787).

An Laura, WoO. 112 (*c.* 1790), to words by Matthisson.

Klage, WoO. 113 (1790), to words by Hölty.

8 songs, Op. 52 (*c.* 1790-92):
  Urians Reise um die Welt, to words by Claudius
  Feuerfarb', to words by Mereau
  Das Liedchen von der Ruhe, to words by Ültzen
  Maigesang, to words by Goethe
  Molly's Abschied, to words by Bürger
  Die Liebe, to words by Lessing
  Marmotte, to words by Goethe
  Das Blümchen Wunderhold, to words by Bürger

Selbstgespräch, WoO. 114 (1792), to words by Gleim.

An Minna, WoO. 115 (1792-93).

Que le temps me dure, WoO. 116 (1792-93), to words by Rousseau.

Traute Henriette (*c.* 1793).

Seufzer eines Ungeliebten and *Gegenliebe*, WoO. 118 (1794-95), to words by Bürger.

Man strebt die Flamme zu verhehlen, WoO. 120 (*c.* 1795).

Erlkönig (sketch for), WoO. 131 (*c.* 1795?).

Adelaide, Op. 46 (1795-96), to words by Matthisson.

4 ariettas and a duet, Op. 82 (1795-96, revised 1809), to words by Metastasio.

Abschiedsgesang an Wiens Bürger, WoO. 121 (1796), to words by Friedelberg.

Opferlied, WoO. 126 (1796, revised 1798), to words by Matthisson. See also choral versions, especially Op. 121b.

Zärtliche Liebe, WoO. 123 (*c.* 1797), to words by Herrosee.

La partenza, WoO. 124 (1797-98), to words by Metastasio.

La tiranna, WoO. 125 (1798).

Plaisir d'aimer, WoO. 128 (1798-1800).

6 songs, Op. 48 (1803), to words by Gellert:
  Bitten
  Die Liebe des Nächsten
  Vom Tode
  Die Ehre Gottes aus der Natur
  Gottes Macht und Vorsehung
  Busslied.

Der Wachtelschlag, WoO. 129 (1803), to words by Sauter.

Das Glück der Freundschaft, Op. 88 (1803).

Gedenke mein, WoO. 130 (1804).

An die Hoffnung, Op. 32 (1805), first setting of words by Tiedge.

Als die Geliebte sich trennen wollte, WoO. 132 (1806), to words by Breuning.

In questa tomba oscura, WoO. 133 (1807), to words by Carpani.

Sehnsucht, WoO. 134 (1807-08), four settings of words by Goethe.

Andenken, WoO. 136 (1809), to words by Matthisson.

Lied aus der Ferne, WoO. 137 (1809), to words by Reissig.

Der Jüngling in der Fremde, WoO. 138 (1809), to words by Reissig.

Der Liebende, WoO. 139 (1809), to words by Reissig.

6 songs, Op. 75 (1809):
  Mignon, to words by Goethe
  Neue Liebe, neues Leben, to words by Goethe
  Es war einmal ein König, to words by Goethe
  Gretels Warnung, to words by Halem
  An den fernen Geliebten, to words by Reissig
  Der Zufriedene, to words by Reissig.

Die laute Klage, WoO. 135 (?1809), to words by Herder.

3 songs, Op. 83 (1810), to words by Goethe:
  Wonne der Wehmut
  Sehnsucht
  Mit einem gemalten Band.

An die Geliebte, WoO. 140 (1811), two settings of words by Stoll.

Der Gesang der Nachtigall, WoO. 141 (1813), to words by Herder.

An die Hoffnung, Op. 94 (1813), second setting of words by Tiedge. See Op. 32 (1805) for first setting.

Der Bardengeist, WoO. 142 (1813), to words by Hermann.

Des Kriegers Abschied, WoO. 143 (1814), to words by Reissig.

Merkenstein, WoO. 144 (1814), to words by Rupprecht. See also duet version with piano, Op. 100 (1814-15).

Das Geheimnis, WoO. 145 (1815), to words by Wessenberg.

Sehnsucht, WoO. 146 (1815-16), to words by Reissig.

An die ferne Geliebte, Op. 98 (1816), song cycle to words by Jeitteles.

Der Mann von Wort, Op. 99 (1816), to words by Kleinschmid.

Ruf vom Berge, WoO. 147 (1816), to words by Treitschke.

So oder so, WoO. 148 (1817), to words by Lappe.
Resignation, WoO. 149 (1817), to words by Haugwitz.
Abendlied unterm gestirnten Himmel, WoO. 150 (1820), to words by Goeble.
2 Austrian folksongs (1820):
   Das liebe Kätzchen
   Der Knabe auf dem Berge.
Der Kuss, Op. 128 (1822), to words by Weisse.
Der edle Mensch, WoO. 151 (1823), to words by Goethe.

Song arrangements with piano, violin and cello
25 Irish songs, WoO. 152 (1810-13).
20 Irish songs, WoO. 153 (1810-13).
12 Irish songs, WoO. 154 (1810-13).
26 Welsh songs, WoO. 155 (1810-14).
12 popular songs of various origins, WoO. 157 (1814-15).
25 Scottish songs, Op. 108 (1815-16).
23 popular songs of various origins, WoO. 158 (1816-18).
12 Scottish songs, WoO. 156 (1817-18).

Symphonies
No. 1 in C, Op. 21 (1799-1800).
No. 2 in D, Op. 36 (1801-02).
No. 3 in E flat, Op. 55 (1803), *Eroica*.
No. 4 in B flat, Op. 60 (1806).
No. 5 in C minor, Op. 67 (1804-08).
No. 6 in F, Op. 68 (1807-08), *Pastoral*.
No. 7 in A, Op. 92 (1811-12).
No. 8 in F, Op. 93 (1812).
No. 9 in D minor, Op. 125 (1822-24), *Choral*.

Overtures
Leonore No. 1, Op. 138 (1805), intended for first performance of *Fidelio*, but abandoned.
Leonore No. 2, Op. 72a (1805), played at first performance of *Fidelio*.
Leonore No. 3, Op. 72a (1806), written for the second version of *Fidelio*.
Coriolan, Op. 62 (1807), overture to a play by von Collin.
Zur Namensfeier, Op. 115 (1815).

Piano and orchestra
Concerto in E flat, WoO. 4 (1784), piano part only survives.
Rondo in B flat, WoO. 6 (1794-95), possibly for the lost first version of the second piano concerto, Op. 19.
Concerto No. 1 in C, Op. 15 (1798).
Concerto No. 2 in B flat, Op. 19 (second version, 1798-1801).
Concerto No. 3 in C minor, Op. 37 (1800).
Concerto No. 4 in G, Op. 58 (1805-06).
Fantasia in C minor, Op. 80 (1808).
(*See* also under **Secular choral music with orchestra**.)
Concerto No. 5 in E flat, Op. 73 (1809), *Emperor*.

Violin and orchestra
Romance in G, Op. 40 (?1802).
Romance in F, Op. 50 (?1802).
Concerto in D, Op. 61 (1806). Also arranged for piano in 1807.

Piano, violin, cello and orchestra
Concerto in C, Op. 56 (1803-04).

Miscellaneous orchestral items
12 minuets, WoO. 7 (1795).
12 German dances, WoO. 8 (1795).
12 minuets, WoO. 12 (1799).
12 German dances, WoO. 13 (c. 1800).
12 *Contretänze*, WoO. 14 (1800-01).
12 *Ecossaises*, WoO. 16 (?1806).
Wellington's Victory, or *The Battle of Vittoria*, Op. 91 (1813).
Gratulations-Menuett in E flat, WoO. 3 (1822).

Items for military band
March No. 1 in F, WoO. 18 (three versions: 1809, 1810 and 1823 with trio).
March No. 2 in F, WoO. 19 (three versions: 1810, 1810 and 1823 with trio).
March in C, WoO. 20 (1809-10).
Polonaise in D, WoO. 21 (1810).
Ecossaise in D, WoO. 22 (1810).
Marsch zur grossen Wachtparade in D, WoO. 24 (1816).

String quintets
E flat, Op. 4 (1795-96). Adaptation of wind octet, Op. 103 (1792). There is a further adaptation of this work for piano, violin and cello, Op. 63.
C, Op. 29 (1801).
C minor, Op. 104 (1817). Arrangement of piano trio, Op. 1, No. 3 (1793-94).
Movement in D minor (1817).
Fugue in D, Op. 137 (1817).
Movement in C (1826). Survives only in a piano arrangement.

String quartets
Minuet in A flat (c. 1794).
2 preludes and fugues (1794-95): No. 1 in F and No. 2 in C.
6 quartets, Op. 18 (1798-1800): No. 1 in F; No. 2 in G; No. 3 in D; No. 4 in C minor; No. 5 in A and No. 6 in B flat.
F (1801-02). Arrangement of piano sonata, Op. 14, No. 1.
3 quartets, Op. 59 (1805-06): No. 1 in F; No. 2 in E minor and No. 3 in C. Razumovsky.
E flat, Op. 74 (1809). Harp.
F minor, Op. 95 (1810).
E flat, Op. 127 (1822-25).
A minor, Op. 132 (1825).
B flat, Op. 130 (1825, new finale 1826).
Grosse fuge in B flat, Op. 133 (1825). Originally finale of Op. 130.
C sharp minor, Op. 131 (1826).
F, Op. 135 (1826).

String trios
E flat, Op. 3 (1792), for violin, viola and cello. Arranged for piano and cello duo, Op. 64.

6 minuets, WoO. 9 (c. 1795), for 2 violins and cello.
Serenade in D, Op. 8 (1796-97), for violin, viola and cello.
3 trios, Op. 9 (1796-98), for violin, viola and cello: No. 1 in G; No. 2 in D and No. 3 in C minor.
Prelude and fugue in E minor (?), for 2 violins and cello.
6 *Ländlerische Tänze*, WoO. 15 (1802), for 2 violins and cello.

String duos
Duett mit zwei obligaten Augengläsern in E flat, WoO. 32 (c. 1795-98), for viola and cello.
Short piece in A, WoO. 34 (1822), for 2 violins.
Canon in A, WoO. 35 (1825), for 2 violins.

Items for wind instruments
3 duets, WoO. 27 (c. 1790-92), for clarinet and bassoon: No. 1 in C; No. 2 in F and No. 3 in B flat.
Duet in G, WoO. 26 (1792), for 2 flutes.
Octet in E flat, Op. 103 (1792), for 2 oboes, 2 clarinets, 2 horns and 2 bassoons. Adapted as string quintet, Op. 4 (1795-96) and trio for piano, violin and cello, Op. 63.
Rondino in E flat, WoO. 25 (1792), for 2 oboes, 2 clarinets, 2 horns and 2 bassoons.
Trio in C, Op. 87 (1794), for 2 oboes and cor anglais.
Sextet in E flat, Op. 71 (1796), for 2 clarinets, 2 horns and 2 bassoons.
Variations in C, WoO. 28 (1796-97), on 'Là ci darem la mano' from Mozart's *Don Giovanni*, for 2 oboes and cor anglais.
March in B flat, WoO. 29 (?1807), for 2 clarinets, 2 horns and 2 bassoons.
3 *Equali*, WoO. 30 (1812), for 4 trombones: No. 1 in D minor; No. 2 in D and No. 3 in B flat.
Adagio (1815), for 3 horns.

Items for strings and wind
Sextet in E flat, Op. 81b (1794-95), for 2 horns and string quartet.
Serenade in D, Op. 25 (1795-96), for flute, violin and viola.
Septet in E flat, Op. 20 (1799-1800), for clarinet, horn, bassoon, violin, viola, cello and double bass.
11 *Mödlinger Tänze*, WoO. 17 (1819), for 2 clarinets, 2 horns, 2 violins and bass.

Piano quartets
3 quartets, WoO. 36 (1785): No. 1 in E flat; No. 2 in D and No. 3 in C.
E flat, Op. 16 (1796). Arrangement of the piano wind quintet, Op. 16.

Piano trios
Movement in E flat (1783).
14 variations on an original theme in E flat, Op. 44 (?).
E flat, WoO. 38 (c. 1790-91).
3 trios, Op. 1 (1793-94): No. 1 in E flat; No. 2 in G and No. 3 in C minor.

Trio arrangement, Op. 63, of string quintet, Op. 4 (1795-96), published 1806.
D (1805). Arrangement of second symphony, Op. 36 (1801-02).
2 trios, Op. 70 (1808): No. 1 in D and No. 2 in E flat.
B flat, Op. 97 (1811), *Archduke*.
Movement in B flat, WoO. 39 (1812).
Variations in G on song *Ich bin der Schneider Kakadu* by Müller, Op. 121a (1815-16).

Piano and violin duos
12 variations in F on 'Se vuol ballare' from Mozart's *Marriage of Figaro*, WoO. 40 (1792-93).
Rondo in G, WoO. 41 (1793-94).
6 Allemandes, WoO. 42 (1795-96).
3 sonatas, Op. 12 (1797-98): No. 1 in D; No. 2 in A and No. 3 in E flat.
Sonata in A minor, Op. 23 (1800-01).
Sonata in F, Op. 24 (1800-01).
3 sonatas, Op. 30 (1802): No. 1 in A; No. 2 in C minor and No. 3 in G.
Sonata in A, Op. 47 (1802-03), *Kreutzer*.
Sonata in G, Op. 96 (1812).

Piano and viola duo
Notturno in D, Op. 42 (?1796). Arrangement of the serenade for string trio, Op. 8 (1796-97).

Piano and cello duos
2 sonatas, Op. 5 (1796): No. 1 in F and No. 2 in G minor.
12 variations in G on 'See the conquering hero comes' from Handel's *Judas Maccabaeus*, WoO. 45 (?1796).
12 variations in F, Op. 66 (1798) on 'Ein Mädchen oder Weibchen' from Mozart's *The Magic Flute*.
7 variations in E flat, WoO. 46 (1801) on 'Bei Männern, welche Liebe fühlen' from Mozart's *The Magic Flute*.
Arrangement, Op. 64, of string trio, Op. 3 (1792).
Sonata in A, Op. 69 (1807-08).
2 sonatas, Op. 102 (1815): No. 1 in C and No. 2 in D.

Piano and mandoline duos
Adagio in E flat, WoO. 43 (1796).
Sonatina in C minor, WoO. 43 (c. 1796).
Sonatina in C, WoO. 44 (1796).
Andante with variations in D, WoO. 44 (1796).

Items for piano and wind
Trio in G, WoO. 37 (1786-87), for piano, flute and bassoon.
Quintet in E flat, Op. 16 (1796-97), for piano, oboe, clarinet, horn and bassoon.
Sonata in F, Op. 17 (1800), for piano and horn.
Serenade in D, Op. 41 (1803), for piano and flute.
Arrangement of serenade for flute, violin and viola, Op. 25 (1795-96).
6 variations (5 on Scottish tunes), Op. 105 (1817-18), for piano and flute or violin.
10 variations on Scottish, Russian and Tyrolese tunes, Op. 107 (1817-18), for piano and flute or violin.

Items for strings, wind and piano

Trio in B flat, Op. 11 (1798), for piano, clarinet or violin and cello.

Trio in E flat, Op. 38 (1802-03), for piano, clarinet or violin and cello.

Arrangement of the septet for wind and strings, Op. 20 (1799-1800).

Piano sonatas

3 sonatas, WoO. 47 (1782-83): No. 1 in E flat; No. 2 in F minor and No. 3 in D.

F, WoO. 50 (c. 1788-90), 2 movements only.

C, WoO. 51 (1791-92), 2 movements only, the second completed by Ries.

3 sonatas, Op. 2 (1794-95): No. 1 in F minor; No. 2 in A and No. 3 in C.

G, Op. 49, No. 2 (1796).

E flat, Op. 7 (1796-97).

3 sonatas, Op. 10 (1796-98): No. 1 in C minor; No. 2 in F and No. 3 in D.

G minor, Op. 49, No. 1 (1798).

C minor, Op. 13 (1798-99), *Pathétique*.

2 sonatas, Op. 14 (1798-99): No. 1 in E and No. 2 in G.

B flat, Op. 22 (1799-1800).

A flat, Op. 26 (1800-01).

E flat, Op. 27, No. 1 (1800-01), *quasi una fantasia*.

C sharp minor, Op. 27, No. 2 (1801), *quasi una fantasia*.

D, Op. 28 (1801).

3 sonatas, Op. 31 (1801-02): No. 1 in G; No. 2 in D minor and No. 3 in E flat.

C, Op. 53 (1803-04), *Waldstein*.

F, Op. 54 (1804).

F minor, Op. 57 (1804-05), *Appassionata*.

F sharp, Op. 78 (1809).

G, Op. 79 (1809).

E flat, Op. 81a (1809-10), *Les Adieux, l'absence et le retour*.

E minor, Op. 90 (1814).

A, Op. 101 (1816).

B flat, Op. 106 (1817-19), *Hammerklavier*.

E, Op. 109 (1820).

A flat, Op. 110 (1821).

C minor, Op. 111 (1821-22).

Piano variations

9 in C minor, WoO. 63 (1782), on a march by Dressler.

6 in F, WoO. 64 (c. 1790), on a Swiss air. For piano or harp.

24 in D, WoO. 65 (first version, lost, 1790; second version, 1802), on 'Vieni amore' by Righini.

13 in A, WoO. 66 (1792), on 'Es war einmal ein alter Mann' from Dittersdorf's *Das rote Käppchen*.

12 in C, WoO. 68 (1795), on 'Minuett à la Viganò' from Haibel's ballet *Le nozze disturbate*.

9 in A, WoO. 69 (1795), on 'Quant'è più bello' from Paisiello's *La Molinara*.

6 in G, WoO. 70 (1795), on the duet 'Nel cor più non mi sento' from Paisiello's *La Molinara*.

12 in A, WoO. 71 (1796), on a Russian dance from *Das Waldmädchen* by Wraniztky.

8 in C, WoO. 72 (1796-97), on the romance 'Une fièvre brûlante' from Grétry's *Richard Coeur de Lion*.

10 in B flat, WoO. 73 (1799), on 'La stessa, le stessissima' from Salieri's *Falstaff*.

7 in F, WoO. 75 (1799), on the quartet 'Kind, willst du ruhig schlafen' from von Winter's *Das unterbrochene Opferfest*.

6 in F, WoO. 76 (1799), on the trio 'Tändeln uns scherzen' from Süssmayr's *Soliman II*. In later editions, the sixth variation was divided into three, making eight in all.

6 in G, WoO. 77 (1800), on an original theme.

6 in F, Op. 34 (1802), on an original theme.

15 and a fugue in E flat, Op. 35 (1802), on a theme from the ballet *The Creatures of Prometheus (Eroica Variations)*.

7 in C, WoO. 78 (1803), on 'God save the King'.

5 in D, WoO. 79 (1803), on 'Rule, Britannia'.

32 in C minor, WoO. 80 (1806), on an original theme.

6 in D, Op. 76 (1809), on a theme from *The Ruins of Athens*.

33 in C, Op. 120 (1823), on a waltz by Diabelli.

Miscellaneous items for piano

Rondo in C, WoO. 48 (1783).

Rondo in A, WoO. 49 (1783).

Minuet in E flat, WoO. 82 (?1785).

Prelude in F minor, WoO. 55 (?1786-87).

2 preludes in all the major keys, Op. 39 (1789).

Lustig-traurig in C major and minor, WoO. 54 (?1790).

2 exercises: No. 1 in C and No. 2 in B flat (c. 1790).

Andante in C (c. 1793).

Minuet in F (c. 1794).

Minuet in C (1794-95).

Three little *Nachahmungssätze* (c. 1794): No. 1 in F; No. 2 in F and No. 3 in C.

Fugue in C (?).

Rondo a capriccio, Op. 129 (c. 1795), *alla ungherese quasi un capriccio*.

6 minuets, WoO. 10 (1795).

Rondo in C, Op. 51, No. 1 (1796-97).

Allegretto in C minor (c. 1797).

Bagatelle in C minor, WoO. 52 (1797).

Allegretto in C minor, WoO. 53 (2 versions, 1796-98).

7 *Ländlerische Tänze*, WoO. 11 (1798).

Allemande in A, WoO. 81 (c. 1800).

Anglaise in D (c. 1800).

Rondo in G, Op. 51, No. 2 (1800).

2 bagatelles (1800): No. 1 in C and No. 2 in E flat.

Canon in G (1802).

7 bagatelles, Op. 33 (1802): No. 1 in E flat; No. 2 in C; No. 3 in F; No. 4 in A; No. 5 in C; No. 6 in D and No. 7 in A flat.

Waltz in C minor (1803).

Canon in A flat (1803).

Theme and variations in A (1803).

Andante in F, WoO. 57 (1803-04), *Andante favori*. Originally slow movement of sonata in C, Op. 53 (1803-04) (*Waldstein*).

Bagatelle in C, WoO. 56 (1803-04).

6 *Ecossaises* in E flat, WoO. 83 (?1806).

Fantasia in G minor, Op. 77 (1809).

2 cadenzas, WoO. 58 (c. 1809), for Mozart's piano concerto in D minor, K. 466.

Cadenzas (c. 1809) for the piano concertos Op. 15, 19, 37, 58 and 61 (arrangement of violin concerto).

Bagatelle in A minor, WoO. 59 (1810).

Ecossaise in G, WoO. 23 (c. 1810).

2 German dances (c. 1811): No. 1 in F and No. 2 in F minor.

Polonaise in C, Op. 89 (1814).

Theme 'O Hoffnung', WoO. 200 (1818), for Archduke Rudolph, who wrote 40 variations on it.

Piece in B flat, WoO. 60 (1818).

Little concerto finale in C (1820), an arrangement of the presto of the piano concerto Op. 37 made for Starke's piano tutor.

Allegretto in B minor, WoO. 61 (1821), for the amateur musician Piringer.

11 bagatelles, Op. 119 (1820-22): No. 1 in G minor; No. 2 in C; No. 3 in D; No. 4 in A; No. 5 in C minor; No. 6 in G; No. 7 in C; No. 8 in C; No. 9 in A minor; No. 10 in A and No. 11 in B flat.

Bagatelle in C (1823-24).

6 bagatelles, Op. 126 (1823-24): No. 1 in G; No. 2 in G minor; No. 3 in E flat; No. 4 in B minor; No. 5 in G and No. 6 in E flat.

Waltz in E flat, WoO. 84 (1824).

Piece of G minor, WoO. 61a (1825), written for Charles Burney's granddaughter Sarah Burney Payne.

Waltz in D, WoO. 85 (1825).

Ecossaise in E flat, WoO. 86 (1825).

Piano duet

8 variations in C, WoO. 67 (1791-92), on a theme by Count Waldstein.

Sonata in D, Op. 6 (c. 1796-97).

Song 'Ich denke dein' by Goethe with 6 variations, WoO. 74 (1799-1804).

3 marches, Op. 45 (1802-03): No. 1 in C; No. 2 in E flat and No. 3 in D.

Fugue in B flat, Op. 134 (1826), arrangement of the *Grosse Fuge* for string quartet, Op. 133.

Organ

Fugue in D, WoO. 31 (1783).

Mechanical instruments

Allegro and allegretto in C for an unspecified instrument, WoO. 33 (?).

3 pieces for a musical clock, WoO. 33 (1799): No. 1 in F (adagio); No. 2 in G (scherzo) and No. 3 in G (allegro).

Grenadiers' march in F (1807-18), for a musical clock.

Select Bibliography

*available as paperback

*Arnold, D. and Fortune, N. *The Beethoven Companion* (Faber, London, 1973 ed.)

Beethoven, L. van *The Letters of Beethoven*, translated and edited by Emily Anderson. 3 vols. (Macmillan, London, 1961)

Breuning, G. von *Aus dem Schwarzspanierhaus* (Schuster & Löffler, Berlin, 1907)

*Kalischer, A. C. *Beethoven's Letters*, with explanatory notes (Dover, New York, 1972)

*Kerst, F. and Krehbiel, E. *Beethoven: the man and the artist, as revealed in his own words* (Dover, New York, 1964)

Kinsky, G., and Halm, H., *Das Werk Beethovens. Thematisch bibliographisches Verzeichnis seiner sämtlichen vollendeten Kompositionen* (Henle, Munich, 1955)

*Landon, H. G. Robbins *Beethoven: a Documentary Study* (Thames & Hudson, London, 1970)

Schindler, A. *Beethoven Biographie*, fifth edition, edited by F. Volbach (Münster, 1927)

*Scott, M. *Beethoven* (Dent, London, 1934, revised J. Westrup 1974)

*Sonneck, O. *Beethoven: Impressions by his Contemporaries* (Dover, New York, 1967)

Sterba, E. & R. *Beethoven and his nephew* (Pantheon, New York, 1954 and Dobson, London, 1957)

Thayer, A. *Ludwig van Beethovens Leben*, translated into German and edited by H. Deiters, then revised and completed by H. Riemann. 5 vols. (Breitkopf & Härtel, Leipzig, 1907–17)

Life of Beethoven, revised and edited by Elliot Forbes. 2 vols. (Princeton University Press, 1964)

Turner, W. J. *Beethoven. The Search for Reality* (Benn, London, 1933 ed.)

Wegeler, F. G. and Ries, F. *Biographische Notizen über Ludwig van Beethoven*, first edition published in Coblenz in 1838, edited by A. C. Kalischer (Schuster & Loeffler, Berlin, 1906)

Index

Acknowledgments

Howards End, by E. M. Forster, from which lines are quoted on p. 135, is published by Edward Arnold, London and Random House, New York. *Point Counter Point*, by Aldous Huxley, from which lines are quoted on the same page, is published by Chatto & Windus Ltd, London and Harper & Row Inc, New York.

The items reproduced were by courtesy of the following collections: Austrian Institute, London 112; Beethoven-Haus, Bonn 17, 34, 36, 64 top left, 64 top right, 64 bottom, 70 bottom right, 84, 89; Bibliotheque Nationale, Paris 73; Dr Marietta Hausknost, Vienna 30; Internationale Stiftung Mozarteum, Salzburg 57 top right; Museen der Stadt Wien 108 top; National Portrait Gallery, London 90; Osterreichische Nationalbibliothek, Vienna 7, 8, 10, 12, 13 left, 13 right, 15, 18, 19, 21, 25, 27, 29 top left, 31, 35 top, 40, 43, 45, 46, 47, 51, 55, 59, 63, 68, 69, 70 top left, 74, 76, 83, 93 top, 93 bottom, 94, 95, 106, 110, 114, 116, 120, 123, 125, 128 bottom; Royal College of Music, London 56; Sammlungen der Gesellschaft der Musik-freunde, Vienna 99 left, 99 right, 126; Stadtarchiv, Bonn 52; Theatermuseum, Munich 104 top; Victoria and Albert Museum, London 60 top.

Photographs were supplied by the following:
Agfa-Gevaert 112; Bavaria-Verlag, Gauting 49, 60 bottom; Bavaria-Verlag – Andy Bernhaut 104 bottom, A. Gruber 97, A. Jungblut 53, Kester Lichtbild-Archiv 29 bottom right, 118, Rolf Mangold 26, K. Meier-Ude 16 bottom, 88, 109 bottom left, Osterreichische Lichtbildstelle 38, P. Stückl 108 bottom; Bildarchiv Foto Marburg 9, 107 top; Bildarchiv Preussischer Kulturbesitz, Berlin 14, 22, 32, 33, 35 bottom, 39, 54 top, 54 bottom, 58, 62, 66, 67, 75, 78, 81 right, 82 top left, 82 bottom right, 87, 100 bottom, 101 top, 102, 103, 117 top, 117 bottom, 124, 128 top, 132; Foto Sachsse, Bonn 52, 64 top right, 64 bottom; Hamlyn Group: Graham Portlock 60 top; Hamlyn Group Picture Library 105, 131; Mansell Collection, London 16 top, 41, 71, 98, 107 bottom, 127, 133; Mary Evans Picture Library, London 23; Arnoldo Mondadori Editore, Verona 61; Radio Times Hulton Picture Library, London 37, 50, 77, 79, 80, 81 left, 111, 115, 121; Snark International, Paris 57 bottom, 100 top; Ullstein Bilderdienst, Berlin 20, 130; Verlag Joachim Blauel, Munich 104 top; Z.E.F.A., London – Anatol 109 right.